INFLATION

INFLATION

by
J. S. FLEMMING

Oxford University Press

Oxford University Press, Walton Street, Oxford OX2 6DP

OXFORD LONDON GLASGOW
NEW YORK TORONTO MELBOURNE WELLINGTON
IBADAN NAIROBI DAR ES SALAAM CAPE TOWN
KUALA LUMPUR SINGAPORE JAKARTA HONG KONG TOKYO
DELHI BOMBAY CALCUTTA MADRAS KARACHI

Casebound ISBN 0 19 877085 5
Paperback ISBN 0 19 877086 3

First published 1976
Reprinted 1977, 1978

Composition by Gloucester Typesetting Co Ltd.
Printed in Great Britain
by J. W. Arrowsmith Ltd., Bristol

PREFACE

MY ORIGINAL intention in writing this book was to produce something suitable to the no man's land between the academic and the lay audience. As the manuscript took shape, however, it became clear that it made demands on readers which would probably restrict it to those who had completed one year of undergraduate economics or had acquired some equivalent familiarity with the subject.

The book was written while I travelled on the train between my home in Oxford and a temporary job at the Bank of England. The contents in no way reflect the views either of my family or of the Bank, although in the course of my work there (which was not closely related to monetary policy) I did learn a certain amount about inflation. I also learnt something from British Rail (especially about the frustrations of queuing behind people who respond rationally—if anti-socially—to high nominal interest rates by paying for their tickets with credit cards) but they too are not to be held responsible for the analysis.

More nearly responsible are my colleagues at Nuffield College, Oxford, and elsewhere, who have stimulated my thoughts and contributed to discussions and arguments. I hope that it is not invidious to pick out Sam Brittan, Max Corden, Nicholas Dimsdale, Martin Feldstein, Herbert Grubel, Richard Harrington, Deepak Lal, John Martin, and Maurice Scott. Their responsibility is clearly limited as few of them have read any of this text.

I am also very grateful to Miss Penny Sylvester whose ability to convert messy manuscript into neat typescript never ceases to amaze those who have encountered my handwriting. My greatest debt is to my wife who cheerfully bore the burdens of coping with four children, whose father was either absent or distracted, at the same time as acquiring first-hand experience of the subject-matter of this book.

January 1976   J. S. FLEMMING

CONTENTS

INTRODUCTION

THIS BOOK is neither a survey nor a critical assessment of alternative simple theories of inflation. I had three reasons for not wanting to write such a book: the first is that it would be redundant because excellent surveys have recently been published.[1] Secondly the interest of simple theories is limited by the inevitable failure of each to account for more than one or two features of the inflationary process. If the theories themselves are all rather unsatisfactory interest tends to focus on the disagreements of their protagonists. What should be a constructive discussion becomes a polarized dispute. This brings me to the third reason for not wanting to write a survey: I believe that there is in fact more scope for agreement and less conflict than is commonly supposed.

My purpose has therefore been to present a synthetic account of the complex inflationary process with its many interacting elements and ramifications. The many facets of inflation make it difficult to reduce the relevant arguments to a single story with a clear thread running through the beginning, middle, and end.

In fact the treatment falls into three parts—of which the first is particularly disjoint. Within each part the development of the argument is relatively continuous; the first, Chapters I–IV, focuses on inflation as a monetary phenomenon. This emerges from the definition of inflation in Chapter I in which the determination of the price level is also discussed in terms which enable us to identify the peculiar characteristics of 'demand pull' and 'cost push' theories of inflation. Chapter II presents a brief summary of the theory of the demand for and supply of money while Chapter III discusses the impact of monetary policy on output and prices and presents the post-war experience of the United Kingdom. Chapter IV considers the implications of the

[1] J. A. Trevithick and C. Mulvey, *The Economics of Inflation*, London, 1975.
 See also D. E. W. Laidler and J. M. Parkin, 'Inflation: a Survey', *Economic Journal*, December 1975.

economy being open to international trade and capital movements. The different effects of monetary changes under fixed and floating exchange rates are emphasized.

The next five Chapters, V–IX, make up the second part of the book, which focuses on the labour market. Chapter V discusses the nature of unemployment without direct reference to inflation. It presents an explanation of the relative importance of price (wage) and quantity (employment) adjustments as firms respond to changing market conditions. This leads to an emphasis on those people who lose their jobs, and modern theories of their job-search are discussed. The employers' search for suitable workers appears in Chapter VI which applies the general labour-market analysis of the previous chapter explicitly to inflation. It relates the notion of (quasi-) equilibria in the labour market to the theory that there exists a 'natural' rate of unemployment such that any attempt to hold unemployment at a lower level leads to accelerating inflation. This acceleration hypothesis relies heavily on the role of price and wage expectations; these are the subject of Chapter VII. If expectations adapt less than instantaneously there exists a trade-off in the short run between unemployment and inflation, or a trade-off between present and future unemployment. Chapter VIII discusses the circumstances in which temporarily high unemployment due to external shocks, such as deterioration in the terms of trade, might make temporary inflation an attractive option. To this point the analysis has been based on the assumption of a competitive labour market. Chapter IX introduces trade unions both as modifying the previous competitive analysis and as possible sources of domestic disturbances comparable to the external shocks considered in Chapter VIII.

Although questions relating to policy choices are raised in Chapter VIII these matters are largely confined to the third part, Chapters X–XIII. Of these four chapters the first two are devoted to an assessment of the costs, and possible benefits, of inflation. Chapter X is restricted to perfectly anticipated inflation, where the costs arise from the failure to, or the costs of, adapting all contracts appropriately, while Chapter XI discusses the costs of uncertainty about future prices; an uncertainty which tends to rise with inflation and to affect the level and especially the nature of investment. The last two chapters are on counter-inflationary policies; the possibility that policies on prices and wages may have perverse effects either on inflation or unemployment is discussed in Chapter XII while the difficulties of a deflationary monetary policy are the subject of Chapter XIII. It is argued there that the two types of policy may be complementary; it is also suggested that when real changes, such as a deterioration of the terms of trade, have contributed to the development of inflation they also affect the appropriate policy response.

Since this work was not designed as a survey, the references in the text are by no means complete. They are supplemented by short bibliographies at the end of each chapter. The works listed are mainly books and selections of articles; as such they often cover much more ground than that of one chapter—none the less each is generally cited only once. For this reason the fact that a particular chapter has few references does not imply that its content is especially original.

I INFLATION, MONEY, AND EXCESS DEMAND

What is Inflation?

THE RATE of inflation in an economy is the rate at which the *general level of prices* in that economy is changing. It is the proportionate change in the general price level per unit of time.

This definition raises two problems: one is related to the idea of a general price level, the second to the rate of change of any price. Consider the price of bread; if a loaf of bread cost 10p in 1970 and 11p in 1971 its price has apparently increased by 10 per cent in one year. But can one be sure that the 11p loaf in 1971 was *qualitatively* identical to the 1970 loaf? Perhaps the proportion of soft to hard wheat has changed, or the baking temperature or the number of slices, or the weight of the wrapping paper. If bread presents so many problems what problems must a TV set or a supertanker present to the statisticians? This problem of measurement is not considered further in this book; we shall proceed as though commodities were unchangeable. It is, however, important to remember that reported inflation rates are based on attempts, inevitably less than perfect, to resolve these serious practical difficulties.

Even if individual commodities do not change their nature the fact that the prices of different products may change at different rates presents difficulties in measuring the rate of inflation. The price of a particular good is the amount of *money* for which one unit of it can be exchanged, the amount of money needed to purchase one unit. If all prices double it is natural to say that the *price level* has doubled, if however some prices have risen by 50 per cent while others have risen by 100 per cent we need a method of combining, weighting, or averaging these changes in order to describe the change in the price level. This can be done by calculating the change in the amount of money required to buy a representative bundle, or basket, of goods and different indices result from putting different goods in the basket. Fortunately the exact composition of the basket is not very important for our purposes, but there are two important distinctions, especially for an economy which engages in international trade. Such an economy is said to be *open*; a non-trading, or *closed*, economy uses only the products of its own activities so that a basket representative of the goods and services produced in the economy is also representative of those used in it, whether for consumption or investment. This is not true of an open economy; some of the things it produces are exported in exchange for imports of goods to be used by its residents, and the *relative price* of imports and exports—its *terms of trade*—are liable to change. Since all economies are open—although some are more open than others—we must choose between an *output price index* and what may conveniently be called a *consumption price index* although it may be argued that it should include goods used for purposes other than consumption.

The discussion which follows refers mainly to the consumption price index which in turn can be taken either including or excluding indirect taxes (and subsidies); the most widely used index in Britain is the *retail price index* which is a tax-inclusive consumption index. Although the price of the chosen basket could be quoted in money terms it is usual to express it as an index number. The cost of the bundle in some particular year, referred to as the base year, is arbitrarily set equal to 100; if the cost rises by 12 per cent over the next year the index rises to 112. It is important that the *rate of inflation is the proportional change of the price index per unit of time*, usually quoted as so many per cent per annum, rather than the absolute rate of change. The absolute rate of change is meaningless as a result of the arbitrariness of the initial value of 100 assigned to the index; a doubling of all prices in a year would raise an index of 10 to 20, or 100 to 200, in each case inflation has occurred at 100 per cent per annum.

The Historical Record

The *retail* price index in the U.K. since 1900 is set out in Fig. 1 line A (this should be read against the right hand scale which takes the price level of 1958 as 100). Line B presents the same data in the form of annual percentage changes (left hand scale). Prices were very stable between 1900 and 1914; they doubled during World War I reaching a level in 1920 which was not reached again until after 1945. From the inter-war nadir in 1934 prices rose fairly steadily at 5 per cent p.a. to double by 1949. They rose sharply at the time of the Korean war

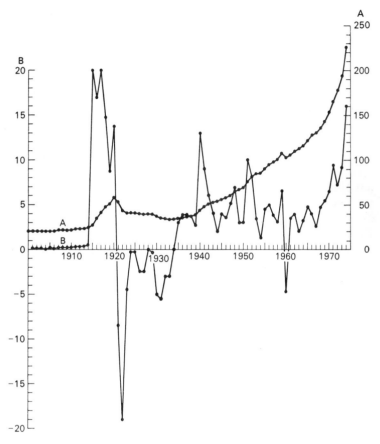

FIG. 1
Source: The British Economy, Key Statistics, London and Cambridge.

and thereafter at a steadily accelerating rate—3 per cent p.a. in the mid-fifties to 10 per cent p.a. in the early seventies. Although the average rate of inflation over the period was low by recent standards, being about $3\frac{1}{4}$ per cent; such is the power of compound interest that prices have risen more than ten times over the seventy-five years. Half of this increase has taken place in the last twenty-five years in which the average rate of inflation has been $4\frac{1}{2}$ per cent.

There are several countries in which prices have risen by a factor of ten over much shorter periods. German wholesale prices rose over 50,000 times between September and December in 1923 alone.[1] This corresponds to a monthly increase of 1,400 per cent. Inflation at this rate was very short lived in Germany but in China inflation ran at over 200 per cent per month (which is about 50 million per cent p.a.) for about a year after six years of inflation at 20 per cent a month or about 800 per cent p.a.[2] These figures make the Latin American rates of 25–75 per cent p.a. seem quite normal. Inflation on the German or Chinese scales, and there have been other examples, is known as hyperinflation. Exactly where the boundary lies between inflation and hyperinflation is obscure but although hyperinflation is an important test of generalizations about inflation it is not the central concern of this book.

Relative Prices and the Price Level

The definition of inflation given above is inconsistent with such usages of the word as 'inflation is more rapid in foodstuffs than in textiles'. Such a description of a situation in which the money prices of both are rising but at different rates is natural to the extent that 'inflation' and 'price increases' are associated with one another. However it is of the essence of inflation, as we shall discuss it, that it refers to the *generality* of prices: what is happening in the situation referred to is that the *relative* price of food and clothing is changing; such a change could occur quite independently of the (inflationary) trend in prices in general. Though conceptually changes in the relative prices of particular commodities are quite distinct from (inflationary) changes in the general price level the two may not be entirely unrelated. We shall see that changes in relative prices, and wages, may contribute to the upward pressure on prices in general. Equally inflation may contribute to the changing pattern of relative prices; for example if the money price of each good is changed infrequently— say once a year—and if different goods have their prices changed at different times of year, then inflation generates an annual pattern of variation in *relative* prices (or wages) on top of other changes which may be taking place. Moreover inflation may redistribute income, or wealth, with effects on demand for, and prices of, different products,

[1] C. Bresciani-Turroni, *The Economics of Inflation: A Study of Currency Depreciation in Post-war Germany*, 3rd English impression, New York, 1968.
[2] H-S. Chou, *The Chinese Inflation 1937–49*, New York, 1963.

while some counter-inflation policies may affect relative wages and relative prices.

Textbooks on 'price theory' do not normally discuss the determination either of the general price level or of the money price of individual commodities, but concentrate on the factors determining relative prices; what, for example, determines the relative price of apples and pears? This is the question to which the theory of supply and demand offers an answer. Suppose that one apple could be exchanged for one pear, in what proportion would people choose to consume them? It clearly depends on their tastes, or preferences, and probably their incomes too. In what proportion would people choose to produce them? It clearly depends on such factors as whether a given quantity of land will yield more apples or more pears, which requires more labour in harvesting and, if the trees flourish in different types of soil, on the relative abundance (and rents) of the different soil types. If, at the hypothetical one-for-one exchange rate people would consume equal quantities but they would produce twice as many apples as pears, then we can say that at this relative price an *excess supply* of apples would exist. It is normally reasonable to assume that people could be induced to increase their consumption of apples, relative to that of pears, by a reduction in their (relative) price, while the same (relative) price change would reduce the output of apples relative to pears. On this assumption the excess supply of apples which existed at the one-to-one exchange rate would be reduced by a fall in the price of apples relative to the price of pears; for example the excess supply might just disappear if one pear could be exchanged for two apples.

The Quantity Theory of Money and Inflation

What does this type of analysis suggest might be the determinants of the general level of prices? We have seen that this can be thought of as the amount of money needed to buy a representative bundle of goods which might itself be thought of as a composite commodity. Thus the general price level can be reduced to a relative price, the relative price of money and the composite commodity. Can we then conclude that the price level is determined by the interaction of people's tastes for money and the composite commodity, on the one hand, and their willingness to produce money and the composite commodity ('output') on the other?

The traditional answer of monetary theorists has been broadly affirmative, but before endorsing a simple 'yes' we must emphasize two problems involved in the application of the simple argument, about apples and pears, to money and output. The first problem is that our story about apples and pears has to be seen in the context of a more general theory in which the relative prices of apples and plums, plums and potatoes, and so on, are all determined simultaneously. Mathematically this problem of *general equilibrium* is not very difficult, at least if one is willing to make a few restrictive assumptions, and the general approach has been familiar since the time of Leon Walras (1834–1910). However this problem is normally formulated by specifying preferences for a list of goods and a technology for their production—money plays no part in the analysis! This omission can be overcome by the simple expedient of including money in the list of goods for which preferences exist, and adding to the technological constraint the statement that the quantity of money is fixed by the monetary authorities.

One cannot, however, leave the matter there for two reasons. One is that some explanation of the place of money in the list of goods—the reasons people have for wanting it—is necessary. One should also check whether the assumptions explaining why people hold and use money are consistent with those underlying the explanation of relative prices, which, as we have seen, does not require the existence of money. The second problem arises from the fact that money is *held* rather than *consumed*, it is a durable good, or asset, like an apple tree, and not a consumption good like an apple. The time dimension is all important here; at a given set of prices I may consume one apple a day and hold £100—the former is a flow, the latter a stock. Thus one cannot consider money without introducing time into the discussion. In the framework of the general equilibrium model this can be done fairly easily, by considering goods at different dates as different goods, and has the effect of introducing intertemporal relative prices i.e. interest rates.

These problems are discussed further in the next chapter, for now we revert to the simple-minded view that if people hold money they must get some use from it—presumably a flow of services of some kind—the quantity of which depends on the quantity of money held. We also assume that people have a demand for these services which is not significantly different from their demand for apples, and a similar argument may be applied to other assets. On this basis we might conclude that the general price level is determined, for given tastes and stocks of assets, by the quantity of money (stock) relative to the available quantity (flow) of the composite commodity. If so a change in the general price level (inflation) must stem either from a change in tastes affecting money holdings, or a change in the quantity of money (or some other asset) relative to the quantity of the composite commodity.

Moreover if we were to assume that labour was always fully employed and that the stock of other assets (land) was fixed the quantity of goods available would be given so that relative availabilities would depend only on the given growth trend in the economy and the growth of the quantity of money. This raises a third important question, 'does the quantity of money ever affect the level of employment, and thus the availability of goods?', for if more money increases the availability of goods it will not necessarily raise prices in the way suggested by the previous argument.

Before taking up these points in the following chapters, it should be mentioned that this basic theory is known as the *quantity theory of money* and is at least 200 years old. It was very clearly expressed by the great Scottish philosopher and economist David Hume who realized that if the quantity of gold coinage in an economy was doubled at the same time that all prices, rents, and wages, in terms of gold, were doubled no real magnitude (relative prices, real weath) would have changed and if the economy was originally in equilibrium its equilibrium would not have been disturbed.

Although this monetary theory of inflation, the holders of which are often referred to as 'monetarists', has an impeccable intellectual pedigree it is by no means universally accepted; other theories, while not attempting explicitly to refute the argument summarized above, rely on such factors as trade-union behaviour, differential productivity change, and disturbances arising from international trade. That each and every one of these factors plays a role in the short run is undeniable. The scheme of this book is to develop a synthetic account of the inflationary process, in which the interaction of these short-run factors with the long-run validity of the quantity theory is exhibited. This involves discussing pressures on the authorities to vary the supply of money in pursuit of the objectives of economic policy—of which price stability is only one.

When discussing the determinants of the *relative* price of apples and pears we referred to the Walrasian hypothesis that relative prices responded to *excess* demands. Prices rise when demand exceeds supply at the going prices and vice versa. Applied to the general price level this reasoning suggests that inflation is generated by an excess of aggregate demand over aggregate supply at the current price; that is, by excess demand for the composite commodity.

Unfortunately this type of inflation theory has acquired the label 'demand inflation' although, as described above, the argument is entirely symmetrical as between demand and supply. On this account, inflation would follow an earthquake, which destroyed a lot of capital goods and reduced output, just as surely as it would follow an increase of demand, at given prices, as a result of monetary and fiscal policy.

It is, however, true that many monetarists not only believe in the excess-demand mechanism but also believe that disturbances to demand arising from monetary and fiscal policy are, as a matter of fact, more commonly the cause of changes in the price level than are autonomous changes in supply. To this extent they can be described as believing in 'demand inflation', or even 'demand *pull* inflation', but it is important to distinguish the two elements of their creed.

Cost Push Inflation

The composite 'demand inflation' doctrine can be rejected as a result of rejecting either of its components. At the micro-economic level one might reject the Walrasian hypothesis that prices respond to excess demands, while at the macro-economic level one might believe that, as a matter of fact, autonomous disturbances to aggregate supply were more important than disruption of aggregate demand whether by the authorities or in other ways.

Both of these positions are known as 'cost inflation' or 'cost push inflation'. These labels cover a number of more specific theories. Several of these are outlined in the following paragraphs and the phenomena which inspire them are considered at greater length in later chapters. In particular many writers emphasize a 'wage push' theory and an 'import push' theory.

The first of these is based on the rejection of the Walrasian price adjustment hypothesis as applying to the labour market. If wages do not respond to excess demand for labour what does determine them? At one level it is sometimes argued that they are determined virtually unilaterally by trade unions. More generally various hypotheses are proposed as to the factors determining trade-union demands. It is suggested that these are related to such things as: the level of the prices paid by workers, tax-induced changes in their take-home pay given their gross wage, the level of their employers' profits, the level of output per employee (productivity), and the level of wages paid by other employers or to other types of workers (relativities).

If these factors simply shifted the supply curve of labour their relevance would be consistent with the Walrasian adjustment hypothesis. In this case the 'wage push' theory becomes the claim that in the labour-market supply side disturbances are sufficiently important to reject narrow 'demand pull' theories but not the general excess-demand theory. The significance of autonomous labour-supply disturbances is considered in Chapter IX where we also discuss the problem raised by the fact that in the presence of trade unions the labour market cannot be described as competitive while the properties of general equilibrium models are well known only for the competitive case.

Thus the 'wage push' theory is only inconsistent with the 'excess demand' theory if the various factors listed above determine wages to the *exclusion of any* effect from excess demand for labour. Excess demand in most markets is very difficult to observe; however, a number of indices do exist in the case of the labour market which enable one to assess the contribution of excess demand to the determination of wages.

A market in which excess demand is not immediately eliminated by instantaneous price responses cannot clear perfectly. Some sellers will be left with unsold stocks or some buyers will have unfilled orders. In the labour market these correspond to unemployed job seekers and unfilled vacancies respectively. Using data on these variables, which of course only approximate ideal measures, one can construct indices of excess demand for labour and relate them to wage changes.

When unemployment alone is used as the index the relationship is often referred to as the *Phillips curve*, after A. W. Phillips who found a significant relationship in data for the period 1861 to 1957 in the

United Kingdom.[3] The rationale for such a relationship is discussed in greater detail in Chapters V, VI, and VII below; what matters here is that although empirical studies of the relationship differ in their degree of refinement, the vast majority of them find that an excess-demand variable *does* affect wage changes; at least this is true of those studies in which any attempt is made to allow for price expectations.[4]

For this reason in what follows the 'wage push' hypothesis will be interpreted not as being inconsistent with a general 'excess demand' theory but as suggesting that in practice disturbances on the supply side of the labour market are very important.[5]

Another 'cost push' theory emphasizes the effect of the price of imports on a consumption price index. Such an index relates to the amount of domestic currency needed to buy a basket of goods which includes some imported items so that the relevant import price is the price of imports in domestic currency. In the case of a small country the foreign-currency price of imports is exogenous but their domestic currency price depends on the exchange rate which may be open to influence by domestic monetary policy as is explained in Chapter IV.

Since for a small country the foreign-currency price of imports, and hence any change in their price, is independent of any domestic excess demand the 'import cost push' inflation theory can again be interpreted as being consistent with a general excess-demand theory, but as suggesting that in practice autonomous disturbances on the supply side of the goods market, specifically affecting the supply price of imported goods, are important.

The simplest 'import cost push' proposition is that an increase in the foreign currency cost of imports contributes to domestic inflation. However, any theory in this area must also tell us whether a fall in import prices is deflationary and also about the effects of changes in the world price of the goods we export. These questions are all considered in Chapter VIII.

[3] A. W. Phillips, 'The Relation Between Unemployment and the Rate of Change of Money Wages in the U.K. 1861–1957', *Economica*, 1958. Laidler and Parkin, op. cit., p. 753, cite some (to) references to the idea of such a relationship.

[4] Price expectations are relevant because it is the *real* wage that should react to excess demand. Expectations are discussed in Chapter VII below.

[5] As noted above the plausibility of this view is examined in Chapter IX below.

Sources and Further Reading

BALL, R. J., *Inflation and the Theory of Money*, London, 1964.

—, and DOYLE, P., (eds.), *Inflation*, Harmondsworth, England, 1969.

BRONFENBRENNER, M., and HOLZMAN, F. D., 'A Survey of Inflation Theory', *American Economic Review*, September 1963; repr. in A.E.A. and R.E.S. Surveys of Economic Theory, Vol. i, *Money, Interest and Welfare*, London, 1965.

BROWN, A. J., *The Great Inflation*, London, 1955.

HANSEN, B., *A Survey of General Equilibrium Systems*, New York, N.Y., 1970.

JOHNSON, H. G., and NOBAY, A. R., (eds.), *The Current Inflation*, London, 1971.

LAIDLER, D. E. W., and PARKIN, J. M., 'Inflation: a Survey', *Economic Journal*, December 1975.

PAISH, F. W., *Studies in an Inflationary Economy—U.K. 1948–61*, London, 1962.

PATINKIN, D., *Money, Interest and Prices—an Integration of Monetary and Value Theory*, Evanston, Illinois, 1956.

TREVITHICK, J. A., and MULVEY, C., *The Economics of Inflation*, London, 1975.

WILES, P. J. D., 'Cost Inflation and the State of Economic Theory', *Economic Journal*, 1973.

WILSON, T., *Inflation*, Oxford, 1961.

II   MONEY: DEMAND AND SUPPLY

The Quantity of Money

THE PREVIOUS chapter suggested that the quantity of money might be a major determinant of the general level of prices and also that changes in preferences, as between money and other assets, or the services of money and other commodities, would tend to change the price level. It is thus very important to be clear what one means by 'money' and to discuss people's motives for holding it. We must then, as suggested above, check that we have not introduced arguments or assumptions inconsistent with the general equilibrium theory underlying the previous discussion.

It should be clear from what has already been said that if there is something which is simultaneously used as a medium of exchange, that is, it is the thing which is usually offered in exchange for commodities in commercial transactions, and which is also the unit in which prices are quoted, then it is money. The problems arise in deciding which assets that people hold should be counted in the *quantity* of the money *stock* in people's hands: that holdings of legal tender (notes and coins) should be included is self-evident—they constitute final discharge of monetary liabilities. The general acceptability of bank cheques, which transfer ownership of bank deposits, as means of payment suggests that we should add the value of current-account balances to the value of notes and coins in circulation when measuring the quantity of money. While theoretical models can be constructed in which the quantity of money is well defined, in practice it is not. Cash can be seen as lying at one extreme of a spectrum of assets which differ in the degree of their 'moneyness'; cash, current accounts, deposit accounts, Post Office savings, national savings, building society deposits, etc. The arbitrariness of a line drawn across this continuum at any particular point renders the relevant concept of the quantity of money somewhat fuzzy. Although this problem may have become more acute with the modern proliferation of financial instruments, even Hume had to draw a line between gold coins and gold ornaments. A doubling of 'all' prices in terms of gold means a halving of the price of gold rings in terms of bread and butter—at least one relative price has changed—and a consequent increase in the non-monetary demand for gold casts doubt on the simple quantity theory.

Wherever we drew the line the same general considerations will determine how much money, thus defined, people will want to hold. These are the money value of the transactions people expect to be undertaking, the cost of holding money rather than non-money assets, and the ease with which non-money assets can be converted into money. Taking these factors in order, we can think of the money value of expected transactions as the product of expected prices and expected real purchases (quantities) which last in turn depend largely on expected, or possibly recent, real income. In this way the money balances people hold tend to vary proportionately with both the level of prices and the level of real income. Another way this can be expressed is that their *real balances*—their money balances adjusted for changes in the price level by dividing by a price index—tend to change in proportion to recent real incomes, other things being equal. In general the total of individuals' demands will depend not only on their total real income but also on the size of the population and the distribution of income.

The Demand for Money

Demand for real balances will vary with the cost of holding them; in the simplest economy, where there is no interest-bearing money, the interest foregone as a result of holding wealth in the form of money rather than, say, bonds is obviously an element of the relevant cost. Unfortunately some monetary aggregates include some interest-bearing assets which confuse the picture, although an interest differential usually exists in favour of the non-money asset. There is no reason to restrict the comparison to other fixed-interest assets; money, if held, is held in preference to pictures, canned food, ordinary shares, and other assets. In principle, there is a margin of indifferent substitution between money and each of these, so that an improvement in the money return expected on any of them would tend to raise the 'cost' of holding real balances and thus reduce the demand for them.

Finally the relevance of 'convertibility' into money applies not only to 'near money' but also to the characteristics of all assets. The more liquid are the forms in which one holds one's wealth the smaller is one's need for cash. Liquidity refers not only to the explicit transaction costs (such as brokerage fees or bank charges for clearing cheques) of converting non-money assets into money, but also to the subjective confidence asset-holders feel they can place in the amount of money that would be realized by liquidation. Thus the demand for money rests on transaction costs and confidence, neither of which figures in the general equilibrium determination of relative prices sketched in Chapter I. While uncertainty can be introduced into the model in a similar way to that suggested for time, the successive extensions of the basic model strain one's credulity: moreover the fact that brokerage fees rise less than proportionately with the size of transactions introduces the problem known in the technical literature as *non-convexity* which might elsewhere be assumed away. The point is that if I can exchange £200 of shares in company A for more than twice as many of B's shares than I could £100, because the brokerage fees are less than twice as large, I would have an incentive to make discrete jumps in my share portfolio even if the underlying factors were moving smoothly. This 'jumpiness' presents analytical problems which have not been solved; one must therefore admit that no *rigorous* basis exists for monetary theory in a general equilibrium context. Despite this *caveat* it seems very likely that the broad qualitative conclusions of the view characterized in Chapter I as 'simple-minded' can nevertheless provide a useful reference point.

The basic proposition of the comparative static quantity theory of Chapter I was that, *other things being equal*, a greater quantity of money would be associated with a higher general level of prices. The preceding discussion of the demand for money enables us to list some of the things which might break this simple link, particularly interest-rate changes and institutional changes, such as more widespread payment of wages by cheque, a shortening of bank-opening hours etc. Consider the established definition of the fairly 'broad' monetary aggregate known as 'M_3' which *includes* not only coins and notes in circulation but also both current, and deposit, bank accounts, but *excludes* deposits with building societies, the Post Office, national savings, etc.[1] A rise in the interest rate paid on bank deposits will increase the demand for 'M_3' by reducing the cost of holding 'money' thus defined, while an increase in the interest paid on building-society deposits will reduce it (in practice these interest rates tend to move together so that the effect of 'the level of interest rates' on demand for 'M_3' may be ambiguous). If banks close on Saturday mornings, or building societies open more convenient offices, one would expect people, on balance, to switch some of their funds from the former to the latter thus reducing the level of demand for 'M_3'.

As an example let us see what would be the consequences for the price level if a shortening of bank-opening hours led people to switch deposits from bank accounts (in 'M_3') to building-society deposits (not in 'M_3'). Since the transfers would be made by cheque the immediate effect would be to transfer the ownership of bank deposits from persons to building societies so that 'M_3' does not in fact fall at once. The building societies have increased deposits matched entirely by liquid claims on banks, they will tend to respond to this situation by increasing mortgage advances and lowering both their advance and their deposit rates. Their increased willingness to make advances will be reflected in the effective demand for houses and either their price or output will rise. Thus the reduced demand for 'M_3' does, even if indirectly, have expansionary or inflationary effects if the supply is not also reduced. The monetary authorities might well make such a reduction if they tried to stabilize interest rates, or the general level of activity, or the price level.

The Supply of Money

When monetary gold was in use the authorities had no control over the money supply; discoveries of gold would increase the supply of money and raise the price, in terms of gold, of other commodities. Nowadays with token coins and paper notes it is the actions of governments and banks that determine the supply. The mere printing of notes would not increase the supply of money because, apart from the printers' overtime payments, the extra notes printed need not get into circulation. The extra notes can get into circulation only if the government spends them or if banks ask for them in exchange for a

---

[1] No particular significance attaches to the use here, and subsequently, of 'M_3' rather than 'M_1' which consists of notes and coins *plus* current bank accounts.

reduction of their accounts at the central bank (the Bank of England). The latter is unlikely to happen in an otherwise settled situation so that further action by the government is necessary to get the money into circulation. The government may issue money to cover a budget deficit when it spends more, either on goods (such as school furniture), services (such as teachers render), or transfers (such as old-age pensions), than it raises in taxation, or for the purchase of financial assets, notably its own debt.

The authorities are always actively managing the national debt, which consists of government securities with various terms to maturity, some of which mature each year. The holders of maturing securities have to be given money, thus if the money supply is not to grow as a result of securities reaching maturity the authorities must sell new securities of equal value to those maturing, but they may not choose to do so. Indeed the authorities can buy in outstanding securities for cash at any time; these transactions, both purchases and sales of debt, are known as 'open-market operations.' If the authorities redeem a maturing stock for cash and make no new issue (or if they make a simple open-market purchase) the holders receive cheques drawn on the central bank, and on paying these into their own banks the latter acquire increased claims on the central bank. A bank's deposits with the central bank constitute 'reserves' against the possibility that depositors may withdraw their deposits; however since such withdrawals by individuals are normally offset by others making deposits, reserves are really necessary only against the small fluctuations associated with the *net* effect of a large number of independent random movements, and the remote contingency of a 'run on the bank'. Thus banks feel that they can safely lend most of the money deposited with them either in the form of purchases of highly liquid short-term government debt, or less liquid advances to private borrowers. The *minimum* ratio of bank money holdings to their deposits is subject to regulation by the authorities.

If the ratio is 10 per cent, the issue by the government of £1m. in cash to redeem maturing debt may add as much as £10m. to 'M_3' because making an advance, or buying government stock, does not reduce the banks' *collective* reserves if the borrower uses the money to pay people who deposit their proceeds with a bank, or if sellers of the government stock again deposit the proceeds. If investing and lending do not reduce the banks' collective reserves, the reserve ratio, which rose as a result of the £1m. injection by the authorities, can be restored to 10 per cent only by an increase of £10m. in their deposits, and this is what happens as a result of their lending or investing. If I deposit £100 with a bank which buys £90 of government stock from someone else his bank deposit rises by £90 and this process can be repeated.

The purpose of this brief excursion into the theory of banking is twofold: firstly it brings out the fact that the relationship between broad and narrow monetary aggregates is not simply one of inclusivity. The narrowest aggregate 'notes and coins' is 'high powered' with respect to the broader aggregates, including bank deposits, because of the multiple effect—through the bank-reserve ratio—of changes in the former. An increase of £1m. in 'notes and coins' might, as in our example, raise 'M_3' not by £1m. (the direct effects of its inclusion in 'M_3') but by £10m. as a result of the reserve-ratio effect. As a corollary of this effect a change in the required reserve ratio by 1 per cent—from, say, 10 to 11 per cent—would tend to reduce bank deposits by 10 per cent even if the supply of 'high-powered money' (notes and coins plus banks' deposits at the central bank) was unchanged.

As mentioned above, the money supply can be increased either by a budget deficit unmatched by borrowing at interest, or by an open-market purchase of interest-bearing debt. In the first case the government must have either cut taxes or raised expenditure, as well as increasing the money supply and it may be difficult to separate the effects of the fiscal aspects of the package from its monetary aspects. For this reason we shall regard open-market operations as the instrument of any distinctively *monetary* policy; a budget deficit unmatched by fixed-interest borrowing can then be described as a combination of debt-financed expenditure *and* an equal open-market purchase, i.e. as a mixture of fiscal and monetary policy.

That open-market operations are the instrument of monetary policy and affect the quantity of money does not mean that the authorities see themselves as following a money-supply policy: that would be implied only if they undertook open-market operations with a view to influencing the money supply. An important alternative reason for them might be to influence interest rates or asset prices. The authorities are in the position of a monopolist facing a downward-sloping demand curve the exact location of which is uncertain. They can either fix the quantity and accept the price thrown up by the market or fix the price and let the market choose the quantity. These are the simple extremes; in practice the authorities have preferences for both prices and quantities. If, at their preferred interest rate, the quantity of money demanded by the market exceeds the authorities' preferred amount they will trade off their two objectives and both the quantity of money and the interest rate will exceed their initially preferred levels.

The authorities' preferences about interest rates may relate either to their level, which they may believe affects aggregate demand (or a particular component of aggregate demand such as investment), or it may relate to the movement of interest rates. They may believe that a policy of trying to control the quantity of money would generate very unstable interest rates with detrimental consequences for fixed investment (or the cost of servicing the national debt). Thus a mixed policy would follow from an attempt to stabilize asset prices.

The Effect of Inflation Expectations on Demand and Supply of Money

Of course, not all 'notes and coins' are available as reserves to banks: some are in people's pockets, piggy-banks, mattresses, purses, and tills. If people reduce their holdings of cash by depositing it with banks the increase in the latters' reserve assets facilitates an increase in the money supply. This kind of change may occur not only when more wages are paid by cheque (perhaps in response to an increase in pay-roll robberies) but also in response to inflation—or rather to inflation expectations. The prospective real return on cash holdings is reduced *pro tanto* by anticipated inflation and it would be reasonable for people to reduce this element in their portfolios and their current accounts at banks in favour of real assets, as well as switching to interest-bearing assets when interest rates change. In this way inflation expectations might increase the reserve-asset base of the banking system. If the banks responded to this situation by lowering interest rates and increasing advances the money supply would increase without any action by the authorities—at least this would be so if inflation expectations were autonomous.

What we have described here is in fact a fall in demand for money as well as an increase in supply in response to expected inflation. This clearly tends to make such expectations self-fulfilling as the rise in the supply of money relative to demand for it tends to raise the equilibrium price level. As the demand for money falls, as well as the supply increasing, the equilibrium price level rises by more than the induced increase in the supply of money. This implies a fall in real balances. If the inflationary process does not reduce real incomes a fall in real balances implies a rise in the *income velocity of circulation*. This is the ratio of real income to real balances or, equivalently, of money income to money supply.

An important question is whether the logical possibility of inflation expectations which justify themselves by raising the velocity of circulation threatens the stability of the whole system. Could a rumour about the prospect of 5-per-cent inflation in a stable economy lead to rapid inflation, a rise in expected inflation, a further fall in demand and an increase in supply of money, more rapid inflation, and so on without limit? The answer depends on the responsiveness of the excess supply of money to the expected rate of inflation and on the responsiveness of those expectations to the experience of inflation. Even if expectations respond quickly and fully to inflation—which, though not the normal situation, can, as we shall see in Chapter VII, be induced by inflationary experiences—empirical studies on countries with both modest inflation and hyperinflation suggest that the responsiveness of the excess supply of money to the expected rate of inflation is far too low to make spontaneous instability a real problem.[2]

This is not to deny that the *velocity of circulation* of money does vary with the rate of inflation. This is particularly notable under hyperinflation. For example in Germany the velocity of circulation in October 1923 was about *eighteen* times as great as in 1919; in 1919 inflation was running at a little over 150 per cent *a year*, by October 1923 it was running at over 1,400 per cent *a month* (i.e. prices were multiplied fifteen times each month).[3] In China the velocity of circulation, measured by the turnover of bank deposits, rose fivefold when the *monthly* inflation rate rose from about 25 per cent in 1946 to about 250 per cent in 1948.[4]

Sources and Further Reading

ARROW, K. J., and HAHN, F. H., *General Competitive Equilibrium*, San Francisco and Edinburgh, 1971.

[2] Laidler and Parkin, op. cit., pp. 747–8.
[3] Bresciani-Turroni, op. cit., pp. 440–2.
[4] H-S. Chou, op. cit., p. 20.

BAIN, A. D., *The Control of the Money Supply*, Harmondsworth, England, 1970.

CLAYTON, G., GILBERT, J. C., and SEDGWICK, R., (eds.), *Monetary Theory and Policy in the 1970's*, London, 1971.

CLOWER, R. W. (ed.), *Monetary Theory*, Harmondsworth, England, 1969.

GOODHART, C. A. E., *Money Information and Uncertainty*, London, 1975.

JOHNSON, H. G., *Inflation and the Monetarist Controversy*, Amsterdam, 1972, — and NOBAY, A. R., (eds.), *Readings in British Monetary Economics*, Oxford, 1972.

KEYNES, J. M., *The General Theory of Employment, Interest and Money*, London, 1936.

LAIDLER, D. E. W., *The Demand for Money: Theories and Evidence*, Scranton, Pa., 1969.

NEWLYN, W. T., *The Theory of Money*, Oxford, 1962.

ROBERTSON, D. H., *Money*, Cambridge, 1930.

III MONEY, OUTPUT AND PRICES IN THE SHORT RUN AND THE LONG

THE BASIC theory sketched in the preceding chapters is explicitly a general *equilibrium* theory: arguably such theories are of no relevance to actual experience since the economy is never in full equilibrium, even instantaneously. To maintain the relevance of equilibrium theory one has to believe that the economic system is *stable* in that it has a tendency to move towards equilibrium. This equilibrium 'target' is however liable to shift from time to time as a result of the impact of unexpected events outside the particular economy in question. If these random shocks are statistically distributed in any reasonable way the assumption that the economic system is stable implies that it will be within a certain 'distance' of equilibrium for a certain proportion of the time. The concept of 'distance' used here has to be a generalization to cover the many characteristics of an economy at each point in time; but, continuing with the one-dimensional metaphor, the implication is that if the economy's equilibrium follows a certain path, there is a band around that path within which the economy will be found, say, 90 per cent of the time. It follows from this argument that the long-run changes of a stable economy are likely to be dominated by changes in its equilibrium position; that is, we can use equilibrium arguments as the basis for analysing long-run trends in an economy which we believe to be stable even if we do not believe that it ever reaches equilibrium.

Thus if one can accept the stability assumption one can describe the quantity theory as applying to long-run trends in the economy. Figure 2 shows the level of money supply, 'M_3', money national income (gross, at market prices) Y, and the general index of retail prices, P, in the United Kingdom for the period 1952–74. The patterns of each of the time series parallel one another in that they all accelerate rapidly after 1969. However money national income and prices have tended to rise respectively somewhat more and less rapidly than the money supply. The fact that prices have risen less fast than money income simply reflects the growth of real income. The fact that money income has grown faster than money supply implies that the ratio of money income to money supply has risen. As was noted above, this ratio is known as 'the velocity of circulation of money'. The velocity of circulation of M_3 was 1·93 in 1952 and 2·35 in 1974, an increase of 22 per cent over the twenty-two years. This increase in the velocity of circulation reflects several factors, including the increase in nominal interest rates, which raised the opportunity cost of holding money, and rising real income per head, which may not require a proportionate increase in individuals' money holdings.

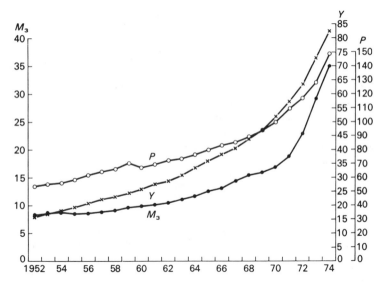

Fig. 2

Sources: Money National Income *Y*—National Income Blue Book; General Index of Retail Prices; Key Statistics, op. cit.; Money Supply, M_3, Bank of England.

With this qualification the parallelism of the trends, even over the fairly short post-war period, is quite striking; however one should bear in mind two caveats. The 'test' of the importance of money implicit in this figure is simultaneously too strong and too weak. It is too strong in that it makes no allowance either for the factors just mentioned as affecting the velocity of circulation, or for the institutional factors referred to in the previous chapter. Moreover the relationship between 'M_3' and the price level depends on the level of real income which does not follow a smooth trend. The 'test' is too weak in that even if Figure 2 is held to be *consistent* with the long-run quantity theory it in no way *proves* its correctness. The *correlations* reflected in such a figure say nothing about the direction of *actual causation* and even less about *possible* causal relationships.

There are certain patterns of behaviour by the authorities, a passive, or *accommodating*, response of the money supply to the demand for money at a given interest rate which imply that the money supply is an effect rather than a cause of other changes. However, even if the correlation over a particular period is historically explicable in terms of the accommodating policy of the authorities, it may still be true that the relationship would survive the adoption of a more active monetary policy. Indeed the fact that the correlation is observed to have held in a large sample of different countries and different times, across which the authorities' activity/passivity with respect to the money supply has not been constant, lends some support to the 'monetarist' view that the correlation does, in some cases, reflect causality running from the money supply to prices and output, and therefore probably *potential* causality in the same direction in others.

Thus we see that the quantity theory offers us a simple and plausible hypothesis about the relationship between the money supply and the price level in the long run. The short-run relationship is illustated in Figure 3, which shows the annual percentage changes in the series shown in Figure 2 (p. 26, above) and also the level (not the change) of the unemployment rate. Figure 3 reveals a much more confused situation than Figure 2; reasons for the absence of any simple relationship in the annual differences will emerge from the discussion below of the short-run response to monetary disturbances. The inflationary process as we know it is the product of a government economic policy formulated day by day, or budget by budget, with rather short-term considerations in mind. It is therefore important to trace out the consequences, in the short run, of a once-for-all increase in the money supply over and above the increase required by the growth of real output.

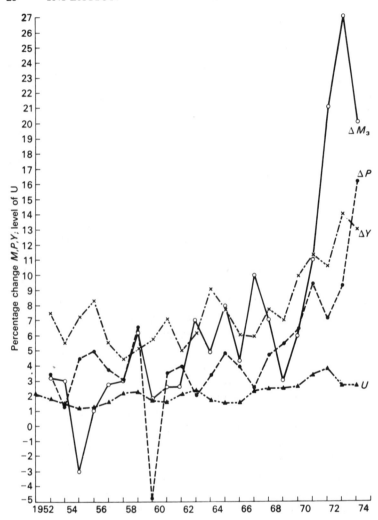

Fig. 3
Sources: as Fig. 2; the U.K. unemployment rate, Key Statistics, op. cit.

The Effects of an Increase in the Money Supply

Whether the motive is to increase the money supply or to reduce interest rates, or to prevent them from rising, the money supply is increased by the government buying in some of its outstanding debt in exchange for which the sellers will receive cheques which, when presented and cleared, will increase not only their own bank deposits but their banks' deposits at the central bank. As these are an important part of the bank's reserves of liquid assets both the sellers of securities and the banks are more liquid than otherwise. At an unchanged interest rate the banks would want to convert some of this extra liquidity into less liquid, and more profitable, investments such as advances to customers. An increase in the money supply thus tends to reduce interest rates. There are several reasons why a reduction in interest rates should increase demand for output; not only does it encourage investment, by raising the present value of future profits relative to present costs, but also, with higher prices for all claims on future income (stocks, shares, houses, etc.), people will be wealthier and likely to spend more of their income.

Unfortunately the empirical evidence on these effects on spending is not at all clear cut. The reason for this is that we have been discussing the effect on expenditure of the hypothetical fall in interest rates associated with an open-market purchase of securities, *other things being equal*. To test this prediction of theory some method of allowing for changes in other relevant things is required. Modern econometrics is quite good at making these allowances as long as the 'other things' are fairly objective, observable, and measurable, and do not regularly accompany the change the effects of which are at issue. Unfortunately neither of these conditions holds; a number of subjective elements, including the expectations discussed above, are very relevant in the present context. If the authorities pursue a policy designed to dampen interest-rate fluctuations, interest-rate falls, in response to other stimuli, will be associated with reductions in the money supply—others things will not have been equal. This failure of other things to be equal is also obvious in the case in which the monetary expansion occurs as a result of a budget deficit, since it is difficult to disentangle the monetary effects from those of the tax or expenditure changes that accompanied it.

As an example of the first problem, consider the case of fixed investment, notoriously affected by the optimism of entrepreneurial expectations. Other things being equal an increase in optimism will increase the demand for investment and bid up the interest rate. If we are to identify a negative effect of independent interest-rate changes on investment we must first make sure that we can allow for the positive association of investment and interest rates generated by autonomous changes in expectations. While considerable progress has been made in this respect it is almost inevitable, by the nature of the case, that the job is inadequately done, and in any historical data the positive association due to unexplained expectational changes may well swamp the negative association due to monetary policy.

In this situation, where the evidence is inevitably inconclusive, it may be held that the belief that monetary policy affects expenditures through interest rates requires an act of faith. If so, it should be noted that far from being a case of 'credo quia absurdum' it is a case of believing an eminently plausible proposition endorsed by nearly all economists up to, and including, Keynes.[1] Moreover this belief is maintained not in the face of strong counter-evidence but in a situation where the evidence is weak and inextricably confused.

The quantity of money is equal to the volume of output times the price of output divided by the velocity of circulation. Thus an increase in the money supply must do one of three things. It might raise output by generating excess demand, as suggested above, or, conceivably, it might raise the price level directly (a possibility which becomes more realistic in an open economy with a floating exchange rate, as is argued in Chapter IV). If neither of these happens then the velocity of circulation must fall, which, other things being equal, it would if interest rates fell. Thus if we rule out the direct effect of money on prices one can ask whether the fall in the interest rate following a monetary expansion has a larger proportionate effect on demand for output or on the demand for money.

Some monetarists have concluded from empirical work that the demand for money is not responsive to interest rates and therefore that aggregate demand *must* respond to the supply of money.[2] More recent studies show that the demand for money is interest elastic but not to the extreme degree which would eliminate an effect on aggregate demand.[3]

Price and Quantity Responses in Fix- and Flex-Price Markets

If then, it is accepted that monetary expansion will increase the

[1] It is true that Keynes did not expect investment to respond much but that was because of inelasticity in the supply of capital goods. Keynes, op. cit., pp. 135, 136.
[2] Notably M. Friedman, 'The Demand for Money—Some Theoretical and Empirical Results', *Journal of Political Economy*, 1959.
[3] See Laidler, op. cit.

level of aggregate demand, in money terms, in this way, we still have to allocate the change in the money value of demand between a quantity change and a price change. Hicks has introduced the terms 'fix-price' and 'flex-price' to characterize markets which respond to demand changes by changing quantities and prices respectively.[4]

In a market in which each week's output was auctioned off on Fridays an unanticipated increase in the money value of demand would be reflected entirely in price changes because supply would be fixed. This is the flex-price case. In practice most industrial products are sold at advertised prices by stock-holding outlets. In this case the initial impact of an increase in demand falls on retailers' stocks. Since retailers tend to work to conventional margins they are unlikely to raise their prices as long as they can obtain supplies from manufacturers at unchanged prices. Manufacturers also hold stocks and, even if their costs of production rise with output, they may not raise output at once, preferring to meet the extra demand by running down stocks; even when they do raise output it is quite likely that if they can buy materials, and hire labour, at unchanged prices, and wages, their costs will not rise significantly. Indeed, as for retailers, an increased throughput at fixed margins increases the return on fixed capital unless capacity is a binding constraint. Thus manufactured products tend to fit the fix-price model, at least in the short run.

In the long run the price of the output of fix-price manufacturers cannot be independent of the prices of raw materials which, like agricultural commodities, are traded on flex-price markets. The long-run response of industrial prices also depends on what happens in the market for their labour input (which is discussed more fully in Chapters V, VI, and IX). In the absence of general involuntary unemployment employers will not typically be able to increase their work force in a competitive labour market without offering higher wages, if only as an overtime premium. If, however, trade unions have negotiated wages in particular industries at which firms face an excess supply of labour, and if only the unemployed actively seek these jobs, an increase in the number of jobs offered by employers will reduce unemployment in the fix-price manner.

Thus the system responds initially to an increase in demand by

[4] This distinction was introduced in J. R. Hicks, *Capital and Growth*, Oxford, 1965, p. 28. It was subsequently applied in the present context in J. R. Hicks, *The Crisis in Keynesian Economics*, Oxford, 1974.

increasing the sales and output of manufactures at unchanged prices; employment rises at unchanged wage schedules but the prices of flex-price commodities rise. Because these are volatile anyway manufacturers will tend to iron out fluctuations in commodity prices when deciding on prices for their own products, so that even the commodity-price rises are unlikely to be passed on in full at once.

However this situation is unsustainable; ultimately three things will undermine it. The increased level of output implies a higher level of money income, even at unchanged prices, which will increase the demand for money, tending to make interest rates rise again and thus dampening the initial stimulus to demand. The increased commodity prices will, if maintained, eventually be reflected in product prices. Finally the sectors of the economy employing workers at a competitive, market-clearing wage will tend to lose labour to the premium employers in the general process of labour turnover. This loss of labour can only be made good by bidding up the competitive wage, which should anyway have risen in line with any increase in prices.

The important point about this story is that an increase in monetary demand is likely to be met, initially by an increased volume of output and only later by increased prices, which stay up even when output reverts to its original trend level. Moreover, as the length of the story suggests, the process may be long drawn out and the possibilities of speculative anticipation may make the delay rather erratic.

The Scope for Speculation

Speculative anticipation would tend to accelerate the process described above, but, depending as it does on expectations, it is unlikely to operate very systematically as far as timing is concerned. The interest rate relevant for most real investment decisions is an interest rate adjusted for the expected rate of inflation—the *real* rate of interest. If the price of bricks, or tinned salmon, is confidently expected to rise by 10 per cent over the next year, one can make a profit of 10 per cent, less storage costs, merely by holding them for resale, or use, at the end of the year. Thus at a given nominal interest rate a higher expected rate of increase of prices stimulates demands for durable goods with low storage costs, and probably fixed investment as well. Thus a monetary expansion, which both lowers nominal interest rates and raises the price level expected to rule in two years' time, is a double stimulus to demand, which tends to make the price increase occur sooner. The working of this mechanism depends on people's consciousness of the link between current monetary changes and future price changes; this consciousness probably varies from time to time, tending to rise with experience of inflation. Thus the delays in the process are initially long, but, if a series of inflationary episodes follow one another fairly rapidly, the process by which monetary expansion is translated into price increases is likely to be less long drawn out each time. Hence Friedman's dictum that the lags in the process are not only long but variable.[5] Indeed inflation may even be caused by the mere expectation of inflationary expansion; this possibility indicates the difficulty of testing the monetary theory of inflation sketched here by finding out statistically whether money-supply changes typically precede, or follow, changes in real output, money income, and prices. Even if income changes first the subsequent monetary change may not reflect passive accommodation by the authorities but be an autonomous change on their part already correctly anticipated by the market.

In all fairness one should also add that there is a symmetrical argument for the case in which the statistics show money-supply changes preceding income changes. In Chapter II we suggested that the demand for money reflected people's (and firms') expected, or planned, expenditures; if therefore an autonomous upsurge of optimism were to increase planned expenditures at the going interest rate the demand for money would increase, tending to raise interest rates unless the authorities were to accommodate the increased demand by increasing the money supply. When the planned expenditure was subsequently made income would rise and it might be tempting to attribute to the preceding increase in the money supply a causal role when it is in fact merely an effect, under accommodating authorities, of a more fundamental change.[6]

Sources and Further Reading

BAILEY, M. J., *National Income and the Price Level*, New York, N.Y., 1962.
DAVIDSON, P., *Money in the Real World*, London, 1972.
ECKSTEIN, O., (ed.), *Econometrics of Price Determination*, Washington, D.C., 1972.

[5] M. Friedman, 'The Rôle of Monetary Policy', *American Economic Review*, 1968.
[6] See P. Davidson, 'Keynes' Finance Motive', *Oxford Economic Papers*, 1965.

FRIEDMAN, M., (ed.), *Studies in the Quantity Theory of Money*, Chicago, Illinois, 1956.

—, and SCHWARTZ, A., *A Monetary History of the United States 1867–1960*, Princeton, N. J., 1963.

MEISELMAN, D., (ed.), *Varieties of Monetary Experience*, Chicago, Illinois, 1970.

NEILD, R. R., *Pricing and Employment in the Trade Cycle*, Cambridge, 1963.

ROWAN, D. C., *Output Inflation and Growth*, London, 1968.

WALTERS, A. A., *Money in Boom and Slump*, London, 1970.

IV THE OPEN ECONOMY

IN CHAPTER I we mentioned that if gold were the only money there would be a connection between gold output and the domestic price level. What exactly is this mechanism? What counterparts exist to it in the absence of a gold standard? and what other differences are there between inflation in open and closed economies?

Consider a country using gold as money but producing none. The country does not trade with its neighbours because they produce the same goods at the same prices. In one of the neighbouring countries gold is discovered in a cheaply extractable form. This represents an increase in wealth for the foreign finders of the gold who will presumably choose to consume more, build themselves bigger houses, and work and produce less.

Thus at the initial price level there will be an excess demand for goods and services which will drive up prices measured in terms of gold. This effect will not be restricted to the country in which the gold is found, as the finders, like other people, will buy where prices are lowest (after allowing for transport costs). However an *immediate* increase in all prices in proportion to the increase in the world stock of monetary gold would not restore equilibrium. This is because the gold would no longer be distributed between the countries in proportion to the value of their incomes and transactions, and thus to their demand for money. If prices are driven up over a period in our country the demand for money, at a given level of interest and output, also increases; this increase can be met by imports of gold in exchange for exports of other commodities. Thus our economy would experience an increase in both prices and money supply, but the causal sequence would be one of joint response to the increase in world money supply rather than a simple response of domestic prices to domestic money. This example also illustrates the proposition that a balance-of-payments surplus is inflationary, and its converse that a deficit is deflationary: the imports of gold in the course of the adjustment process are not treated as commodity imports but as the monetary counterpart of a trade surplus.

Fixed Exchange Rates

The situation would be very little altered by the absence of commodity money if exchange rates between national token moneys were rigidly fixed, and people were utterly confident that they would be maintained. In this case the world, and domestic, price level is determined by the sum of national money supplies. Any one country's increase in its money supply will only raise prices in the proportion that it adds to world money supply.

Notice, however, that if there were ten countries each with 100 units of money outstanding and one increased its money supply by 10 per cent (10 units) the world money supply, and thus prices, would rise by only 1 per cent—but this means that domestic demand for money would increase by only 1 per cent. Thus nine of the extra money units must be circulating abroad, in which case foreigners must have exchanged them for goods. This highlights the impossibility of such a system: it can only work as long as foreigners are willing to accept our money as being as good as theirs.

The fixed-exchange-rate systems which have existed did not involve any commitment by foreigners to accept others' money, but a commitment by the authorities in each country to give foreign currency in exchange for their own. This means that the commitment to a fixed exchange rate involves a restriction on the ability to increase the domestic money supply. If a small country, with a fixed exchange rate, increases its money supply more rapidly than its neighbours (after allowing for differences in real growth rates) the open-market purchases will in effect be from foreigners since nothing has changed the domestic demand for either money or bonds. As our currency thus accumulates in the hands of foreigners their confidence in the exchange rate is weakened by the growth of their potential claims on our unchanged reserves of foreign exchange. If they demand that our authorities honour their pledge to maintain the exchage rate, by giving foreign currency in exchange for their holdings of ours, then the authorities' reserves of foreign currency will be depleted and their ability to sustain their commitment jeopardized. Thus a real commitment to maintaining its exchange rate requires that no country expand its money supply too fast.

The consequences of slow expansion are less damaging to the honour of the authorities since the large reserves resulting from importing inflation through a trade surplus do not pose the threat to confidence in the sustainability of exchange rates that vanishing reserves represent. For this reason real commitment to fixed exchange rates, and competitive determination to maintain reserves, might well lead to a deflationary bias in world money supply, as each country's authorities attempted to ensure that its own money supply expanded less rapidly than the total.

The situation of a large country in such a system is rather different. If one country does half the world's trade it is natural that other countries should choose to hold about half their foreign exchange reserves in that country's currency as long as it is assumed to be stable. If every country has holdings of this currency it is likely to be used to finance trade with third countries and the demand for it may well rise above 50 per cent of total exchange reserves. In this situation a devaluation of the major currency is unlikely to be a matter of indifference to its trading partners for three reasons; first it reduces the value of their reserves in terms of the quantities of third-country imports they command, secondly it is likely to accelerate inflation in the large country, thus reducing the purchasing power there of holdings of its currency, and thirdly it represents an increase in the competitiveness of an important rival and thus jeopardizes the countries' own surplus position. The minor countries are therefore likely to be ambivalent in their attitude to the major country's exchange rate and this may make them reluctant to press for conversion of their holdings for fear of precipitating a devaluation. This fear and this reluctance present the dominant country with an opportunity to enrich itself at the expense of its neighbours. If it expands its money supply it will run a trade deficit, i.e. it will be able to consume more than it produces, which implies that other countries produce more than they consume. They can avoid the payment of this tribute only by revaluing their currencies or demanding conversion of their reserves either of which would precipitate a capital loss. In this situation the authorities in the dominant country may well at some stage attempt to exploit their position (possibly accidentally) which, for a while, will involve their domestic inflationary policy generating a worldwide inflation.

Flexible Exchange Rates

At the other extreme from commitment to fixed rates, with the necessity that countries hold official reserves of foreign exchange, is a system of freely floating rates which, in its purest form, implies that countries hold no *official* reserves at all, though some private people may hold foreign currency for speculative reasons or to balance their porfolios. If this demand is small the floating-rate system approximates to the closed-economy case with two provisos. The first of these is that expected real interest rates will tend to be equated in all countries if capital markets are free. In this situation a country's exchange rate will tend to change at the rate at which its inflation rate differs from that of other countries, while its inflation rate will be related to the rate of domestic monetary expansion as in the closed-economy case. The second qualification is that the time pattern of responses in an open floating economy may, as we shall see, be very different from a closed one.

Between these extremes of exchange-rate system lie the 'adjustable peg' fixed-rate system established at the post-war Bretton Woods conference and the 'managed floating' rate system into which it was transformed between 1971 and 1973. Both of these systems allow for exchange-rate changes but at the initiative of the authorities rather than that of the market. Under the 'adjustable peg' system each country commits itself to maintaining its exchange rate within a small margin on either side of a *par value* fixed in terms of some other currency, or mix of currencies, *for the time being*, but is free to vary its par value from time to time. Since these changes are infrequent they take the form of discrete steps; in this respect the adjustable peg differs from a 'managed float' under which the authorities are not committed to maintaining any particular exchange rate, even in the short run, but choose to hold reserves so as to be able to influence the market rate day by day.

Thus, under the adjustable peg, devaluation is not unthinkable and countries may be willing to risk that consequence of an expansionary monetary policy. A more interesting question is whether, if most countries are inflating, any one country can resist the impact of world inflation by revaluation of their currency. Under the adjustable-peg system such revaluations would have to be relatively infrequent; this has two unfortunate consequences for the country trying to pursue a stable price policy in defiance of the trend of world prices. First the periodic revaluations are liable to become anticipated and lead to currency speculation with a consequent disruption of the whole system. Secondly the discrete adjustments, when they occur, involve a temporary loss of profitability in export, and import-competing, industries. Naturally this gives rise to lobbies and pressure groups which will try to make the authorities delay the revaluation. The longer this is delayed the greater the upward pressure on prices and the more nearly the country's inflation rate will be brought into line with world rates.

Thus, compared to a rigid commitment to fixed rates, an adjustable-peg system reduces the deflationary bias, while as compared to a freely floating system, it makes standing out against an inflationary trend more difficult. It also shares the problems discussed above created by any one country's currency being a large part of others' reserves.

The preceding summary theoretical analysis of alternative international monetary arrangements has considered in the abstract a number of special cases to which the perceptive reader will probably have already given names: the large country whose currency is so widely held as a reserve that it could extract international tribute by causing world-wide inflation in a fixed-rate system is the United States of the late 1960s. The country bravely struggling to maintain price stability in the same period is Germany whose currency appreciations were subject to much speculation and internal dissension.

Price and Quantity Responses Under Floating Exchange Rates

Although lip-service was given to price stability as an objective of economic management throughout the post-war period of quasi-fixed exchange rates, the effective constraint on expansionary policies, which it was hoped would raise the rate of economic growth—'going for growth'—was seen, at least in Britain, in terms of the balance of payments. One reason for the balance of payments playing this constraining role, and thus displacing price stability as even a secondary objective of policy, follows from the analysis given in Chapter III of the consequences of monetary expansion. There it was argued that quantity effects would precede price effects in a closed economy. In an open economy with a fixed exchange rate much of the initial increase in demand following a monetary expansion would be met from increased imports and reduced exports. These combine to worsen the balance of payments on current account even if negligible price changes occur. Thus the balance of payments can be seen as a constraint on the expansion of demand without any reference to intervening effects on prices.

Under freely floating rates the effect of expansion is very different; apart from deficits which may be covered by private capital movements, the current account must balance under a 'clean', unmanaged, float. In this situation demand expansion affects the price level by inducing a fall in the exchange rate and this effect is likely, for two reasons, to be much quicker than in the closed-economy case discussed above. First the foreign-exchange market is just the kind of flex-price market referred to there; and now when the initial increase in demand for goods spills over into increased demand for imports, and reduced supply of exports, it is translated into a change in the balance of supply and demand for foreign exchange, and hence in the exchange rate. This effect will quickly lead to an increase in the prices of all tradable goods if the exchange devaluation is not considered transitory.

This brings us to the second reason for a quick price response; exchange-rate changes are unlikely to be regarded as transitory by importers and exporters because in their experience speculators successfully even out most predictable fluctuations. These speculators are well advised professionals who are fully aware of the connection between domestic demand and the exchange rate; they are therefore quite capable of moving the exchange rate down not only in immediate response to expansionary monetary or fiscal policies but even on the basis of their judgement that such policies are imminent.

If this speculative behaviour is important it can generate evidence which obscures the causal mechanisms on which the speculators operate. They believe that excess monetary demand *causes* inflation and devaluation; anticipating an increase in demand they may sell the domestic currency, making the devaluation (and possibly the inflation) *precede* the expansion of monetary demand. With such intelligent anticipation it may almost become necessary to speak of effects preceding their causes. This confusion is not restricted to price effects: the anticipation of inflationary policies which depresses the exchange rate will thereby stimulate demand both for exports and import substitutes, though these quantities may adjust relatively slowly to the devaluation. Thus not only may price effects precede the monetary expansion but they may also precede the output response—a complete reversal of the sequence described in the closed economy where the speculative switches-out of money were into fix-price goods rather than into flex-price foreign exchange.

This reversal, as a result of which price changes may precede monetary changes, is liable to be interpreted, as noted above, as revealing a non-monetarist causal chain, in which the money supply is responsive rather than responsible. However, on the argument presented here, that interpretation is misleading—the possibility that price and output changes precede monetary changes does not imply any weakening of the basic monetarist insight since the speculation which causes the reversal is itself based on that theory, and profitable. By the pragmatic/empirical criteria applied by Friedman's 'Chicago school' the profitability of acting *as if* a theory were true, is very strong support for it.

What would happen if the foreign-exchange market falsely anticipated a monetary expansion? Would their false expectations generate pressures for changed policies leading to their fulfilment? Suppose the market anticipates a monetary expansion when none is intended; the exchange rate falls, this increases the demand for exports, which respond slowly, and raises the price of imports which work through the system fairly quickly. Will this generate unemployment and thus political pressure to increase the money supply in line with the foreign-exchange markets' expectations rather than the government's original intentions? The answer depends on the responsiveness of money wages. In the extreme case they might rise as soon as the exchange rate fell and before industrial prices rose. In this unlikely case real wages would rise, tending to generate unemployment and hence pressure for monetary expansion. In the more plausible cases real wages would fall, and demand for labour would rise, so that a government which regulated the money supply in line with labour-market pressures, would actually reduce the money supply as a result of a chain of reactions to a widespread belief that they would expand it. Thus even if a slight permanent increase in prices did emerge one could hardly say that the market's expectations were self-fulfilling; indeed although speculators may be able to cause a little extra inflation in this way they will certainly lose money in the process. It is therefore unlikely to occur very frequently.

The consequences of changing the exchange system can be

illustrated by the British experience after the pound was floated in June 1972. There seems to have been a feeling that floating the pound removed the balance-of-payments constraint on growth and neither its past role as a proxy for price stability (at least relative to other countries), nor the more rapid impact of demand on prices under the new system, was recognized.

Sources and Further Reading

ALIBER, R. Z., (ed.), *National Monetary Policies and the International Financial System*, Chicago and London, 1974.

CONNOLLY, M. B., and SWOBODA, A. K., *International Trade and Money*, London, 1973.

HINSHAW, R., (ed.), *Inflation as a Global Problem*, London, 1972.

MUNDELL, R. A., *Monetary Theory: Inflation, Interest and Growth in the World Economy*, Pacific Palisades, Calif., 1971.

PARKIN, J. M., and ZIS, G., (eds.), *Inflation in the World Economy*, Manchester, 1975.

V UNEMPLOYMENT AND THE LABOUR MARKET

IN PRINCIPLE there exists a competitive general equilibrium pattern of employment and real wages which is parallel to, indeed determined simultaneously with, the equilibrium pattern of output and relative prices discussed in Chapter I. This model emphasizes the role of the availability of labour of different talents, the opportunities for converting talents into skills by training, the preferences of people for the consumption of goods and of leisure, and the possibilities of using the various skills in alternative combinations with one another, and with the available land and capital equipment, to produce different goods. These factors determine an equilibrium allocation of labour to regions, industries, products, and techniques; it follows from the definition of such an equilibrium that everyone willing to work at the going rate for his skill would have a job—in equilibrium there is no unemployment, although some people may choose not to work.

Unemployment is associated with disequilibrium. Disequilibrium results from unanticipated change—change not necessarily anticipated by nobody, but taking somebody by surprise. Such surprises are disequilibrating in a world where information is incomplete, expectations differ, and the many markets necessary to reconcile these expectations do not exist. In this chapter we discuss the way in which disequilibrium might generate unemployment even in a competitive economy—the implications of monopolistic firms and especially labour unions are the subject of Chapter IX.

The unemployed constitute a pool of unutilized labour and it is convenient to analyse the determinants of the size of the pool into those affecting the inflow and those affecting people's length of stay once they enter. The inflow consists of two components; new entrants to the labour force, school-leavers, mothers returning to work and such-like (who are largely offset by hirings to replace those dying, retiring, or leaving to have children), and those whose becoming unemployed represents a *separation* from their previous job. Separations in turn may, from the employee's point of view, be either voluntary (resignations or 'quits') or involuntary (sackings).

Keynes distinguished between *voluntary* and *involuntary unemployment*,[1] of which the latter was distinguished by being responsive to the level of aggregate demand. Our division of separations is not equivalent to Keynes's distinction but the latter has not been found very useful in practice, perhaps because, as we shall see, unemployment will always respond, other things being equal, to an increase in demand.

While the level of voluntary labour turnover is high, especially when unemployment is low, this is not a very significant factor in explaining unemployment because voluntary movers stay unemployed for only a short time, if indeed they register at all. Thus the level of unemployment which should concern us is determined by the inflow of new entrants to the labour force, the level of *involuntary separations,* and the amount of time such people spend searching for jobs. The duration of such periods of search is affected by the unemployed man who sets his own requirements for an acceptable job. In this sense his unemployment is voluntary and will respond to certain economic incentivies, to which we shall return after discussing the determinants of involuntary separations which clearly occur on the initiative of employers.

Wage Rigidity and Employment Adjustment

It is so common to explain lay-offs in the motor-car or textile industries in terms of 'a downturn in demand' for cars or cloth, that we rarely ask whether the employer had any alternative. Why does he sack men rather than cut their wages and meet the fall in demand by a price cut? One reason for stickiness of wages and prices is the existence of trade-union and producer monopolies, but there are reasons to believe that even in a more competitive labour market employers would very often declare men redundant before trying to reduce relative wages. This is because it typically pays an individual employer facing a reduced demand for his product to sack men rather than to shorten the length of the shift they work.

[1] J. M. Keynes, *General Theory of Employment, Interest and Money*, London, 1936, pp. 6 and 15.

The normal wage agreement specifies an hourly rate, 'normal' hours of work, an overtime premium, and a minimum level of pay—the actual hours worked, at least up to 'normal' hours, being chosen by the employer. Consider an employer operating at normal hours, say fifty per week, with 100 men. His wage bill would fall by 2 per cent if either the work-week were shortened by one hour or if two men were sacked. His choice might therefore depend on which measure reduces output least. A reduction of the work-week by 2 per cent would be expected to reduce output in much the same proportion, a reduction of employment by 2 per cent might well reduce production considerably less. This is partly because machine-hours might be substituted for man-hours, although the scope for this is limited; more important is the possibility of closing down the less productive, less efficient, older machines or plants, at the same time as reducing the level of employment.

Against this argument for adjusting employment when demand changes, must be set the costs of hiring and firing which may induce labour hoarding, at least in the face of what may be believed to be a temporary fall in demand. The reduction in the typical work-week as work is shared between both the necessary and the hoarded workers does not point towards wage flexibility in the way that it would if employers were interested only in the number of man-hours they got for their money, and did not find it more profitable to vary employment than hours. The point is that employers have a preference for long shifts, because they increase the use of the most productive equipment, and are restrained only by the disproportionate expense of overtime and shift working. 'Normal' hours reflect the employers' preferences and will typically be longer than the hours employees would choose at the basic wage rate.

If employers merely specified an hourly wage rate and men could check in and out at will it would hardly be feasible for them to respond to a reduced demand for their product in any way other than by reducing the wage rate. They might conceivably use their records of each man's attendance and try to ration the available work by restricting each man to, say, 90 per cent of the hours he had worked in the previous week, while maintaining the rate of pay. But this procedure obviously involves a restriction on the men's earning opportunities, and it is quite possible—indeed entirely rational—that they should be willing to accept a slight reduction in the hourly wage rate in order to regain unfettered choice over their hours of work and, very probably, a higher expected income.

However, if, as we have suggested is likely, employers have established 'normal' hours *longer* than those workers would choose if given the option of working at the basic hourly rate for hours of their choice, a modest shortening of the work-week, associated with some hoarding of labour, in a recession, would increase their satisfaction, by reducing the discrepancy between actual hours and those desired at the basic wage, and so would not make them at all receptive to suggestion of a wage cut. Thus despite the costs of hiring and firing there is a fundamentally technological reason why a competitive industrial labour market would probably respond to changes in demand by involuntary separations and would not show very great wage flexibility.[2]

The rate of involuntary separation clearly depends on the rate of change of the equilibrium pattern of employment. Changes in the industrial or regional pattern occur for a number of reasons; with a given pattern of prices the demand for some products grows while that for others contracts as a result of income, taste, tax, or demographic change; with a given pattern of demand for products, employment in one industry or firm may decline as a result of the introduction of a less labour-intensive technology; relative product prices may change because international prices change, and this may change the desired pattern of output; payroll taxes or 'incomes policies' may change relative wage costs and this may change the desired pattern of employment.

Consider a situation in which the demand for the product of one industry has increased at the expense of another. Some transfer of employment will probably be necessary, although, if the change is slow enough, a lot can be done by the expanding industry recruiting all the new entrants and the declining industry relying on 'natural wastage'. To bring about a more rapid change than this, or to preserve the age structure of employees in both industries, some workers would have to change jobs. There are two forces that can induce such movements, the attraction of better wages (in relation to working conditions) or the compulsion of losing the existing job.

---

[2] This argument is set out more fully in J. S. Flemming, 'Wage Rigidity and Employment Adjustment', in J. M. Parkin and A. R. Nobay (eds.), *Contemporary Issues in Economics*, Manchester 1975.

For a given rate of change of demand patterns greater flexibility of relative wages would probably be associated with a lower level of unemployment because it is not clear that a man moving in response to wage differentials need ever be unemployed: in principle he can find out about other jobs without giving up his own, and make a switch when he finds a better one.

Thus the quasi-equilibrium, or 'normal', rate of unemployment in an economy tending to follow a shifting equilibrium, depends on the pressure for change in the pattern of employment, pressure arising from changes in the patterns of world prices, demand (as influenced by taxes and other policies), and technology on the one hand, and on the other, on the rigidity of relative wages, and the responsiveness of workers to wage differentials and employment opportunities. This last factor can broadly be described as the mobility of labour but it includes all the determinants of the duration of unemployment in the face of given opportunities.

Mobility, Search, and Unemployment Compensation

Labour mobility depends on several things; the workers' information about alternative opportunities, open-mindedness to change, the general applicability of their skills, and the strengths of family and other social ties which may restrict them to particular areas. In the case of geographical mobility the structure of the housing market is very important; any non-transferable subsidies, including below-market rents such as council and controlled tenants enjoy in Britain, effectively restrict them to jobs within commuting distance of an arbitrarily given 'home base'. Transport costs also affect the economically feasible commuting distance.

These factors affect the set of opportunities an unemployed man will consider, they determine the area of his search rather than his criterion for accepting any particular offer within this area. It is not entirely inconceivable that he should knock on the door of the first employer he finds, ask not 'Have you a job?' but 'What will you pay me?', take it, and continue his search for a better job in his spare time —but this is clearly not what happens. It does not happen for a variety of reasons, one of which is that employers are not geared to taking people off the street and guessing a wage at which it would be profitable to employ them. Employers are engaged in a search for suitable employees which is symmetrical with workers' search for suitable employment. To this end employers advertise wages with a view to generating a flow of applicants from which they can choose those who best meet their requirements. They are used to searching for the man to fit the job specification rather than the job to suit the specific applicant. Another reason is that the job seeker may know that he can search more effectively if he does it full time—the labour exchange keeps normal hours. Moreover some jobs that a man might take on as a temporary stopgap could actually make his subsequent re-employment in his preferred line more difficult—calloused hands may disqualify one from managerial jobs.

The purpose of the search activity of the unemployed is to acquire information by identifying and approaching potential employers. It is clear that such an activity is subject to diminishing returns. While it is unlikely that the first contact will lead to the ideal job on ideal terms it is equally unlikely that the 500th will turn up anything very different from all its predecessors. Thus while planning to spend some time searching is sensible the appropriate period is unlikely to be very long. An important determinant of the amount of time devoted to searching is the cost, in terms of income and leisure foregone, of an extra week's search. An 'unemployed' man may be doing any of three things; actively looking for work; having a rest; or actually working, either in his own garden or decorating his neighbour's house. Whichever way he spends his time he will spend more time 'unemployed' the weaker the income incentive to work. That is, the better the 'unemployed' are paid in relation to the wages they could earn at 'work', the longer will be spells of unemployment and, for given turnover, the higher the level of unemployment.

Moreover it is quite likely that more generous unemployment compensation will increase labour turnover. The counter-argument is that lengthened search leads to a better matching of men to jobs and therefore to less dissatisfaction and less turnover. However this factor is probably outweighed by the fact that generous unemployment compensation makes the security of any job offered less important. That a job is seasonal matters less the more the compensation payable when one is laid off. Generous compensation may not induce matching for life but rather the feeling that one can given an unknown type of employment a try because even if it does not work out little will have been lost.

So far we have assumed that a man laid off believes he has to find a new job; there is evidence from the United States that a very large proportion of such men are normally rehired by their previous employers.[3] This phenomenon is a rational response to the existence of unemployment insurance; employees like stability of employment and income; in the absence of unemployment insurance employers find it pays to hoard labour; paying men for doing nothing when demand is slack is more than compensated by the effect of this policy on the wage necessary to recruit labour. If there is unemployment insurance the employer who lays off his 'hoard' with good rehiring prospects saves the whole of their wages while they lose only about half—the rest coming from unemployment insurance. An employer adopting such a policy can afford to pay higher wages to his men when they are employed than could an employer who kept his 'hoard' on his own payroll. Thus over good times and bad together the employees of the firm adopting a lay-off policy enjoy higher average incomes, longer paid holidays, and no significant loss in long-term job security.

A book on inflation is not the right place for the discussion of the optimal set of unemployment-compensation arrangements and the related question of the optimal level of unemployment. Unemployment could obviously be reduced if the authorities were very beastly to the unemployed but this may not be a sensible policy not only because it is hard on the unemployed. If the unemployed are searching for more suitable jobs it may be that this activity benefits people other than themselves—we may all gain if square pegs are not harried into round holes. At its crudest there is a simple argument arising from the tax system; if a better job means a better-paid job it means a job in which a man contributes more to the public purse through taxation. Since other people thus indirectly share in the fruits of successful job-search it may be entirely proper that they should share in the cost. This is the argument for generous tax treatment of investment in plant and machinery and applies equally to an unemployed man's investment of time in searching for a suitable job.

Institutional and Social Changes Affecting the Normal Rate of Unemployment

There are two points here which are of prime relevance to our dis-

[3] See H. S. Parnes, G. Nestel, and P. Andrisani, *The Pre-retirement Years*, Center for Human Resource Research, Columbia, Ohio, 1972.

cussion of what we called above the 'quasi-equilibrium' rate of unemployment. One is that whether the changes are desirable in themselves or not, one should recognize that a better deal for the unemployed will mean, other things being equal, more unemployed. On the other hand, the more effort put into enforcing the 'active search' and 'reasonable requirement' provisions of the compensation scheme and the more help various official and unofficial placement agencies give to job-seekers, and especially to new entrants to the labour force, the shorter will spells of unemployment be and, other things being equal, the lower the level of unemployment. Secondly the magnitude of this effect depends heavily on social attitudes. If great stigma or trauma is associated with being unemployed then people will look for work even when the prospective increment in their cash income is small—as it often is. However, even if this attitude is the dominant one, the existence of an identifiable subculture dedicated to making the most of the welfare system can have a sizeable impact on measured unemployment when one starts from a level of less than 3 per cent of the work force. There can be no doubt that in many western countries the trend of both these factors has tended to raise the quasi-equilibrium or 'normal' rate of unemployment since the Second World War.

As far as the first factor is concerned Table I gives the ratio of income after tax for an unemployed Briton with a wife and two chil-

TABLE I

U.K. Benefit Ratio Percentage (October each year)[4]

1950	36·5	1960	39·5	1970	72·7
1951	36·0	1961	44·3	1971	77·6
1952	41·5	1962	43·0	1972	73·7
1953	39·3	1963	47·4	1973	70·6
1954	36·7	1964	44·6		
1955	39·4	1965	49·3		
1956	37·1	1966	68·6		
1957	35·5	1967	73·2		
1958	44·0	1968	72·9		
1959	41·9	1969	71·0		

Source: Social Security Statistics 1973, H.M.S.O., London, 1975, p. 207.

[4] The ratio is (standard rate unemployment benefit + earnings related supplement (since 1966) + family allowances) ÷ (average weekly earnings + family allowances − income tax − national insurance contributions).

dren to his after-tax income in employment if his earnings were equal to the weekly average for each year from 1950 to 1974.

Table I shows that, though subject to some variation from year to year, the benefit ratio was stable between 36 and 46 per cent from 1950 almost until 1966 when the introduction of the earnings-related supplement raised the ratio to the 68- to 78-per-cent range. The figures for other groups are broadly similar—the increase for a single man being from about 25 per cent before 1966 to about 50 per cent afterwards. The tendency of benefit ratios to rise is not peculiar to the United Kingdom; for example, between 1966 and 1969 the benefit/wage ratio rose from 43·1 per cent to 51·4 per cent in France and from 25·3 per cent to 37·1 per cent in West Germany.

What are the consequences of failure on the part of the authorities to recognize the implications of more generous unemployment compensation (such as that associated with the introduction of Earnings Related Supplements in the United Kingdom in 1966), or the decline of the 'puritan work ethic'? If for either of these reasons, or for any other reason, the 'normal' rate of unemployment rises, then the level of employment one can call 'full' falls, and so must full-employment output. Thus if equilibrium is to be maintained the authorities must take steps to *reduce* the level of aggregate demand and, if the price level is not to rise, they must reduce the supply of money. Suppose however that they fail to recognize an increase in the normal rate, and that their policy is geared to maintaining an unchanged 'full employment' target; then if their initial target was correct their new target must be too high which carries inflationary consequences as we shall see in the next chapter.

Sources and Further Reading

HILL, M. J., *et. al.*, *Men Out of Work*, Cambridge, 1973.

MAKI, D., and SPINDLER, Z. A., 'The Effect of Unemployment Compensation on the Rate of Unemployment in Great Britain', *Oxford Economic Papers*, November 1975.

PHELPS, E. S., *et. al.*, *The Microeconomic Foundations of Employment and Inflation Theory*, New York, N.Y., 1970.

ROBINSON, J., *Essays on the Theory of Employment*, 2nd edu., Oxford, 1947.

TAYLOR, J., *Unemployment and Wage Inflation*, Harlow, England, 1974.

WOOD, J. H., *How Much Unemployment?*, Institute of Economic Affairs Research Monograph 68, 1972.

WORSWICK, G. D. N., (ed.), *The Concept and Measurement of Involuntary Unemployment*, London, 1976.

VI UNEMPLOYMENT, EXPECTATIONS, AND THE ACCELERATION OF INFLATION

The Natural Rate of Unemployment

THE DEFINITION of the quasi-equilibrium level of unemployment discussed in the previous chapter involved no reference either to money or to inflation. It is, however, virtually identical to the concept of the *natural rate of unemployment* which is central to the monetarist theory of inflation.

We have seen that the determinants of the quasi-equilibrium rate, which include the rate of technological change, the fickleness of fashion, and the generosity of unemployment-compensation schemes, are not all natural forces. However the use of the word 'natural' in this context is not meant to suggest that the rate itself is an immutable natural phenomenon, but rather to associate it with Wicksell's doctrine of the natural rate of interest. Wicksell argued that there was a cumulative process by which any attempt to hold the real rate of interest below the 'natural rate' dictated by the real forces of thrift and the productivity of capital would lead to accelerating inflation.[1] The monetarist argument parallels this exactly, asserting that any attempt to hold unemployment below its natural rate will lead to accelerating inflation. Can we substantiate this assertion?

The first point to make is a negative one: that only constant inflation is compatible with the quasi-equilibrium in which the normal or natural rate of unemployment should emerge. This is because equilibrium requires the fulfilment of expectations and it is plausible that the fulfilment of price-level expectations requires that prices rise at a constant rate—not necessarily zero. It is easy to see how a steady growth of prices would eventually be built into people's expectations and difficult to see how they could correctly anticipate a more erratic progress of prices. The way in which expectations are formed is the subject of the next Chapter (VII).

[1] K. Wicksell, *Interest and Prices* (1898), repr. in English, London, 1936 and 1962.

In Chapters III and IV we argued that whether monetary expansion first affected prices or quantities would depend on the scope for anticipatory speculation. If prices are first affected while money wages, being fixed for discrete periods, are slow to respond, real wages initially fall. In the other case greater utilization of plant may possibly enable producers to reduce prices, or more plausibly, to employ men at higher wages without raising prices. Thus in the second case the real wage might actually rise. This difference between the initial phase of the two cases requires that the account of the reversion of unemployment to its normal level—or of the acceleration of inflation—be presented by way of two distinct stories.

Two Stories

The first story relates to the case in which prices rise first, perhaps as a result of the impact of monetary expansion on the exchange rate as suggested in Chapter IV. With money wages fixed for the duration of current contracts employers find that the real cost of employing labour at the agreed money wages has fallen, and are willing to employ more. Employment increases if the supply is forthcoming. The additional supply comes from a reduction of unemployment. Some of the unemployed will find employers willing to hire them who would previously have said 'no vacancies' and some of these extra opportunities will be acceptable to the job-seekers. They may be acceptable despite the fact that in real terms they are inferior to the offers that might have been, but were not, previously made. There will also be a reduction in involuntary separations as, at the reduced real wage, the decline of contracting industries will be arrested.

This reduction in unemployment cannot be sustained because it depended on a reduction in the real wage from that determined in the market resulting from an *unexpected* price rise. Unemployment can be held at the new low level only as long as prices continue to rise faster than expected, and that is hard to imagine even if inflation is accelerating. It is clearly unlikely that steady inflation at 7 per cent p.a. should continue indefinitely to surprise people to the same extent year after year—this is discussed further in Chapter VII.

The situation is less straightforward in the second case in which the output increase comes first; in Chapter III it was suggested that this is the typical pattern for a closed economy, or under fixed exchange rates. The problem is why firms should increase output in response to an increase in demand at given prices when on our competitive assumption they could always have sold more output at the going price. One explanation is that much of industry is not competitive, another is that in the kind of quasi-equilibrium associated with continuous change, in an economy characterized by incomplete information and incomplete markets, competition takes on a different aspect. In the real world all manufacturers set the prices at which they are willing to sell their products and set a wage they are willing to pay to the labour they need however 'competitive' their business.

An increase in demand leads to increased sales, a reduction of stocks, and a greater demand for labour, as in the previous story. Pressure on product prices comes from two sources, the upward pressure on wages and on prices of raw materials. In this story each firm fixes its wages at a level at which it expects to be able to select the men it wants from applicants willing to work at that wage.[2] If unemployment has been reduced by hirings to meet the recent increase in demand the number of job applicants to each firm at its announced money wage will fall. Moreover if any prices, such as foodstuffs, have risen because of the demand for commodities, and particularly if unemployment benefits are indexed to the cost of living, applicants may demand, that is be willing to search until they find, higher money wages. Thus firms will raise wages in order to restore the situation in which they could readily recruit suitable labour whenever they wanted to, and these higher wages will be passed on in higher prices. At any rate of unemployment lower than the normal or natural one this mechanism will generate rising wages. Moreover if money wage offers are fixed for a period, such as a year, firms anticipating wage increases by other firms will take them into account when setting wages. Thus, as in the previous story, unemployment can only be held below its normal level if monetary demand is persistently unexpectedly high, which implies unexpectedly rapidly rising wages, and almost certainly accelerating inflation.

In these two stories both employers and employees recognize the reality of their present position; they are induced to behave 'abnormally' by the combined effect of infrequently revised money wages and incorrect price- and wage-level expectations. It is not necessarily true that they will recognize the reality of their position; this applies

[2] See R. E. Hall, 'The Process of Inflation in the Labour Market', *Brookings Papers on Economic Activity* 2, 1974.

particularly to employers whose perception of their situation is influenced by accounting conventions. The effect of these conventions, which are discussed more fully in Chapter X in connection with taxation, is to overstate the rate of profit in a time of inflation. This arises from the inadequacy of the historic-cost depreciation charge, the inclusion of the appreciation of stocks held in trading profits, and the undervaluation of capital employed.[3]

To the extent that the employers' perception is distorted by these accounting conventions they are likely to employ labour, pay (real) wages, and invest, in excess of the (quasi-) equilibrium rates. This factor then contributes to the acceleration of inflation by stimulating demand. It is not likely that accelerating inflation would enable the process to continue; on the contrary the more rapid the increase in inflation the more quickly managers will recognize the inadequacy of their accounting conventions. When this happens firms will simultaneously cut back on investment and employment while trying to raise prices relative to wages. This, of course, further diminishes the sustainability of the initial fall in unemployment which was enlarged by the exaggeration of accounting profits.

Does the Natural Rate Vary with Inflation?

While we have tried to substantiate the monetarist claim that attempts to hold unemployment below some critical level, which itself depends on a variety of real factors, leads to accelerating inflation, we have in no way substantiated the implicit claim that this critical level is independent of the rate of inflation. There are at least four ways in which it seems possible that inflation *does* affect the natural rate.[4] Two of the more plausible relate to wage rigidity. Some of the forces of wage rigidity apply peculiarly to downward movements of the *money* wage, and were therefore ignored in the previous chapter. Keynes concentrated exclusively on this aspect, although he explained it in terms of an anxiety not to fall behind other people's

[3] F. Sandilands (Chairman), *Inflation Accounting*, Cmnd. 6225, H.M.S.O., London, 1975. A. Glyn, and R. Sutcliffe, *British Capitalism, Workers, and the Profits Squeeze*, Harmondsworth, England, 1972.
[4] The factors considered above are effects of monetary conditions on the labour market. Some factors, such as an increase in the dispersion of rates of productivity growth, may, on some assumptions about wage behaviour, raise the natural rate of unemployment, and, under certain monetary policies, also the rate of inflation.

wages. This type of wage rigidity becomes less relevant the faster the rate of inflation; downward stickiness of money wages ceases to constrain movements of relative real wages—one can become relatively worse off simply because one's money wage rises relatively slowly.

This phenomenon would tend to make the natural rate of unemployment fall with more rapid inflation, but the second process has the opposite effect. This is the tendency of inflation to strengthen trade unions, a tendency which is discussed in Chapter IX: one explanation of this tendency is that as long as wage agreements are in simple money terms (i.e. not linked to a price index) inflation means that agreements will be more shortlived. Negotiation is time-consuming and if it becomes more frequent it is not surprising that specialist groups of negotiators undertake an increasing proportion of negotiations. Moreover some unorganized workers may fall behind in the process of inflation and their discontent makes them more willing to be organized. These two linkages probably make the natural rate fall with modest rates of inflation (less than 5 per cent p.a.) but rise with higher rates.

The other two feedback effects which both relate to the duration of job-search are even less certain. In principle job-search is an investment activity in that present income from a less attractive job is sacrificed in the hope of finding a better job conferring future benefits. Thus like all investment activities it should be sensitive to the rate of interest. If, as is often the case for reasons to be discussed in Chapter XI, interest rates do not rise to match the rate of inflation, the real cost of borrowing, or dissaving, to finance search activity falls, and one might expect unemployment to rise. On the other hand the level of unemployment compensation may not be indexed, in which case as inflation progresses the ratio of compensation to the wage falls, which should tend to reduce unemployment. Of these two effects the former may not be very significant if the unemployed have neither savings nor access to the capital market, while the latter is probably most significant at low rates of inflation—at higher rates such benefits are among the first things to be linked to either a price or a wage index.

If we could conclude that, though the natural rate of unemployment may vary as between different rates of steady inflation, such variation is probably unimportant in practice, there is a fairly simple method of estimating the natural rate. If there exists in the historical record any considerable period over which (i) the rate of inflation showed no trend, (ii) the rate of unemployment showed no trend, (iii) fluctuations in both were small, and (iv) the real factors contributing to the natural rate were fairly constant, then the rate of unemployment in that period was the natural rate for that period.

Figure 3 in Chapter III shows unemployment and inflation over the period 1952–74, and Table I in Chapter V shows the benefit/wage ratio over a similar period. The conditions above were all met, with respect to these variables, over the period 1952–65. Condition (iv) is uncomfortably open-ended. Ignoring other possibly relevant factors, such as regional policy and modest incomes-policy, the figures suggest that the natural rate of unemployment was then between $1\frac{3}{4}$ and 2 per cent; it has probably risen since 1966 for the reasons mentioned at the end of Chapter V.

Sources and Further Reading

BRITTAN, S., *Second Thoughts on Full Employment Policy*, London, 1975.

FRIEDMAN, M., 'The Rôle of Monetary Policy', *American Economic Review*, March 1968.

—, and LAIDLER, D. E. W., *Unemployment Versus Inflation*, London, 1975.

KAHN, R. F., *On Re-reading Keynes*, Oxford, 1975.

LAIDLER, D. E. W., and PURDY, D., (eds.), *Labour Markets and Inflation*, Manchester, 1974.

PERRY, G. L., *Unemployment, Money Wage Rates and Inflation*, Cambridge, Mass., 1966.

PHELPS, E. S., *Inflation Policy and Unemployment Theory: the Cost-Benefit Approach to Monetary Planning*, New York, 1972.

TOBIN, J., 'Inflation and Unemployment', *American Economic Review*, March 1972.

VII THE BEHAVIOUR OF PRICE LEVEL AND INFLATION EXPECTATIONS

IN EACH of our two basic stories, in which misperception played no part, acceleration of inflation followed from hypotheses about the role and behaviour of expectations. It was assumed, first, that money bargains are made in terms which reflect the parties' expectations as to their real value. The second assumption was that steady inflation would eventually be reflected fully in expectations—that people's price and wage expectations cannot be consistently falsified by inflation. Both these propositions are simple corollaries of the economist's habitual assumption that people are *rational*. Since money is useful only for what it will buy it is only the expected real value of a given money wage that is relevant. Rational people must be assumed to learn from their experience: indeed the 'rational expectations hypothesis' postulates that on average, and in the long run, people's expectations will be fulfilled.[1]

Rational and Adaptive Expectations

In fact there are two versions of the 'rational expectations hypothesis'. In its stronger form it asserts that a theorist who assumes that economic agents are rational must believe that their expectations are derived from the theory he himself believes to be supported by the evidence. On this basis a monetarist is required to assume that other people's price expectations are based on recent changes in the money supply while someone who believes that wages or import prices lead consumer prices should assume that people's expectations of the latter are related to recent experience of the former.

In this form the hypothesis is far too strong—though it does provide a useful check on the long-run viability of a theory. In the short

[1] J. F. Muth, 'Rational Expectations and the Theory of Price Movements', *Econometrica*, 1961. T. J. Sargent, and N. Wallace, 'Rational Expectations and the Dynamics of Hyperinflation', *International Economic Review*, 1973.

run one theorist can, and often does, believe, with no inconsistency, that other people's behaviour is influenced by their acceptance of the teaching of false prophets. The weaker rational expectations assumption only implies that the false prophet will be revealed and recognized, *in the end*, for what he is. Moreover it is perfectly consistent to hold a theory that theorizing is difficult and costly and therefore that non-specialists will rationally form their expectations on the basis of rules of thumb. Their 'rationality' only implies that a rule of thumb will be abandoned if it is shown to be consistently wrong.

While the strong 'rational expectations hypothesis' is too strong it is certainly suggestive of a model appropriate to markets, such as financial ones, which are dominated by experts and professionals. Indeed as 'the efficient market hypothesis' it has been found to be consistent with the evidence in a number of recent studies of financial markets.[2] The labour market is probably not such a market and certainly would not be under competitive conditions: it therefore seems fruitful to consider the kind of rules of thumb that people might adopt who wanted to learn from their experience without aspiring to professional status.

In this chapter we concentrate on the inferences about future prices that people might draw from observation of past price movements. This rather incestuous pattern of inference can, as we shall see, be made quite sophisticated, but even if people do use rules of thumb they need not be of this type. They may believe that particular events have implications for prices, that prices rise after devaluation, or that they rise faster when unemployment is low. These beliefs point either towards the stronger 'rational expectations hypothesis' or towards rather complicated fistfuls of rules of thumb. Our emphasis on the family of incestuous rules does not imply any denial that other patterns of inference are at work and may well be important in particular episodes.

The simplest and most popular model of learning in this context is that known as the *adaptive expectations* hypothesis which postulates that expectations are revised in proportion to their current error. Thus a man who had on Monday expected the temperature on Tuesday to be 70° might, on finding it to be 66°, revise his forecast

[2] See E. F. Fama, 'Efficient Capital Markets: a Review of Theory and Empirical Work', *Journal of Finance*, May 1970.

for Wednesday to 68°. In this example he gives equal weight to his expectations for, and the outturn on, Tuesday in forming his forecast for Wednesday.

Consider a variable subject to random influences which are not related to one another in successive periods, so that its value at any particular time is the sum of a constant *normal* value and a random term which is expected to be zero, but might be either positive or negative. If one knew with certainty that the normal value was constant, and that the random term in each period was independent of that in other periods (so that a positive random term on one day made a positive random term the next neither more nor less likely), then the best forecast one could make would be one's best estimate of the variable's normal value. This would be the simple arithmetic mean, or average, of its past observed values. However if one thinks it possible that a variable's 'normal' value may be trending in either direction, or if it is possible that one day's being hot makes it more likely that the next one will be so, then the best forecast will be an average of past values giving disproportionate weight to recent experience.

It is shown in the Appendix to this chapter that the adaptive expectations procedure is equivalent to such a weighting scheme. If, as in the example above, one has systematically given equal weight to one's last forecast and to the out-turn in forming one's next forecast, then one's forecast will in fact be an average of the values of past observations with weights $\frac{1}{2}$, $\frac{1}{4}$, $\frac{1}{8}$, etc. Thus if the Tuesday temperature of 66° had been preceded by 72° on Monday and 68° on Sunday our man's forecast for Wednesday would be

$$\tfrac{66}{2} + \tfrac{72}{4} + \tfrac{68}{8} + \ldots = 59\tfrac{1}{2} + \ldots$$

since these last three days contribute only $\frac{7}{8}$ of the total weight put on past experience the earlier experience which has a weight of $\frac{1}{8}$ must itself have an average value of 68° to bring the forecast for Wednesday up to 68°. If one gives $\frac{2}{3}$ of the weight to one's previous expectations and only $\frac{1}{3}$ to the most recent observation the expectation will be a weighted sum of past observation with weights $\frac{1}{3}$, $\frac{2}{9}$, $\frac{4}{27}$ . . . .

The case in which equal weight is given to the current observation and the previous expectation can be illustrated graphically, as in Figure 4. If X_0 and X_0^e are the values of X at time zero, and the value expected to rule then, respectively, X_1^e is constructed to lie halfway between them. If the actual value of X at time 1 is X_1, X_2^e can be constructed similarly and so on.

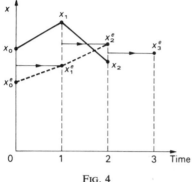

FIG. 4

As long as the variable being forecast has no trend this adaptive procedure will generate 'forecasts' which are unbiased in that on average they are correct, they simply smooth out random fluctuations. If, however, the variable tends to rise, it is shown in the Appendix that the forecast will tend not only to fall behind the actual value at the time to which the forecast refers, but also to be smaller than the most recent observations when the forecast is made. People applying this procedure to a variable which rises steadily would always be expecting its next value to be lower than its present one. Under this procedure forecasts only rise if they have previously been too low and will only rise steadily as long as they stay too low.

Despite this shortcoming of the adaptive expectations process it does capture some aspects of learning in a particularly neat and simple way. It allows one to combine in a specified way the accumulated experience embodied in one's previous expectation with the information provided by one's new information. How can this procedure be reconciled with the requirement of the 'rational expectations hypothesis' that expectations be right on average in the long run?

A Synthesis

The consideration of a very different problem may suggest an answer to this question in the context of inflation do the relevant expectations relate to the *level of future prices*, or the *rate of change of prices* (the level of the rate of inflation), or to the *rate of change of inflation* or to its *acceleration*, or to some even higher order characteristic of the process?

We noted above that the procedure implied that people had some notion of a 'normal' value for the variable to which it is applied from which they expected only temporary deviations to occur. Thus it would seem appropriate to apply the formula to the price level itself if people's reaction to a price increase is to expect prices to fall back towards their original level; to apply it to the rate of inflation if they react to its acceleration[3] by expecting a return towards the normal rate of inflation, and so on. How people actually react in various circumstances we do not at the moment know, but it is clear that to avoid persistent error the formula should not be applied to a variable which has a trend.

Even if the price level or the rate of inflation has a trend, and therefore is unsuitable to the adaptive expectations procedure, there will be a higher-order variable which does not (yet) have such a trend. Thus the issue would be resolved if the adaptive expectations formula were applied only to orders of differences (or derivatives) which showed no trend. Indeed we can invoke Occam's razor to suggest that in the interest of simplicity people apply the adaptive expectations formula to the *lowest-order* difference (or derivative) of the inflation process to have shown no trend in recent years.

If the price *level P* has shown no trend then the forecast of next period's price is a combination of the expectation held last period about this period's price level and the actual price level now. If however people know that there has a been a trend in prices in recent years they will look at the ratio of prices in successive periods (P_t/P_{t-1}) which is closely related to the rate of inflation — with inflation at 10 per cent per period $P_t/P_{t-1} = 1\cdot1$.

If the rate of inflation has not shown any trend people will forecast next period's *inflation* rate by combining last period's expectation and out-turn. They then forecast next period's price *level* by applying this expected inflation rate to the current price level. It should be clear that while the adaptive mechanism applied to price levels would make

---

[3] Strictly speaking, to describe rising inflation as 'accelerating' is to confuse inflation, the proportionate rate of change of the price level, with the price level itself: increasing inflation implies acceleration of the price level.

people respond to inflation by expecting prices to fall the process applied to the rate of inflation involves people in projecting a price trend related to their recent experience.

It may, of course, be that the rate of inflation itself reveals a trend. If inflation is accelerating, forecasts based on the extrapolation of recent trends will consistently underestimate future prices and, on our rationality hypothesis, people will start to forecast prices by the ratio of successive price ratios $((P_t/P_{t-1})/(P_{t-1}/P_{t-2}) = P_t P_{t-2}/P^2_{t-1})$.

In principle this scheme can be extended to higher orders of differences, or ratios, as circumstances may require, although it is difficult to imagine operating beyond the third level. The most important feature of this generalized system, which integrates both the adaptive and rational expectations hypotheses, is that it attributes to expectation-forming processes what may be called 'changes of gear'. These occur whenever people realize that the variable on which they have been operating adaptively is subject to a trend. A downward change of gear depends on realizing that the next variable down the hierarchy is *not* subject to a trend: to this extent the changes are asymmetrical and the process not simply reversible. When such a 'change of gear' takes place in an upward direction there is an exceptionally large increase in the expected price level as people's idea of normality changes from the price level of a previous period to the rate of inflation of that period applied to the current price level. Indeed this change in forecast price level will be greater than that generated by consistent operations in either 'gear'.

Two Examples

Some of the characteristics of applying the different levels of the adaptive expectations procedure are demonstrated in the following examples. In both cases it is assumed that prices are constant at 100 until year 1. In case A they then start oscillating 95, 105, 95, 105 ... while in case B they then start rising at 5 per cent a year 105, 110·25, 115·76, 121·55. Whether operating in first or second gear equal weight is given to the current observation and the previous expectation.

We denote actual prices at time t by the variable P_t and the prices expected at time $t-1$ to rule at time t by $_iP^e_t$ where the index i refers to the relevant 'gear'. I_t and $_iI^e_t$ are corresponding actual and expected inflation rates.

CASE A: 'FIRST GEAR':

In year 1 P_1 and $_1P_1^e = 100$ so that $_1P_2^e = 100$.
In year 2 $P_2 = 95$ so that $_1P_3^e = (P_2 + _1P_2^e)/2 = 97\cdot500$.
In year 3 $P_3 = 105$ so that $_1P_4^e = (P_3 + _1P_3^e)/2 = 101\cdot250$.
In year 4 $P_4 = 95$ so that $_1P_5^e = (P_4 + _1P_4^e)2 = 98\cdot125$.

CASE A: 'SECOND GEAR':

In year 1 I_1 and $_2I_1^e = 0$ so that $_2I_2^e = 0$ and
             $_2P_2^e = P_1(1 + _2I_2^e) = 100$.
In year 2 $I_2 = -5\%$ so that $_2I_3^e = (I_2 + _2I_2^e)/2 = -2\cdot5\%$ and
             $_2P_3^e = P_2(1 + _2I_3^e) = 92\cdot625$.
In year 3 $I_3 = +10\cdot5\%$ so that $_2I_4^e = (I_3 + _2I_3^e)/2 = +4\cdot0\%$
             and $_2P_4^e = P_3(1 + _2I_4^e) = 109\cdot214$.
In year 4 $I_4 = -9\cdot5\%$ so that $_2I_5^e = (I_4 + _2I_4^e)/2 = -2\cdot8\%$
             and $_2P_5^e = P_4(1 + _2I_5^e) = 92\cdot383$.

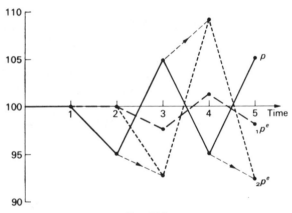

FIG. 5(a)

The actual and expected prices for this case are shown in Figure 5(a). The dashed lines with arrows on them represent the construction of the second gear expectations. Clearly in this case of oscillating prices the more stable first gear is to be preferred; not only are the initial errors smaller but they diminish slightly over time while the second gear errors actually get slightly larger. If the price level continues to oscillate systematically—as it might over the seasons—no adaptive procedure is any good. Even on the weak version of the rational expectations hypothesis people should learn about simple repetitive processes.

Case B: 'first gear':

In year 1 P_1 and $_1P_1^e = 100$ so that $_1P_2^e = 100$.

In year 2 $P_2 \rightleftharpoons 105{\cdot}000$ so that $_1P_3^e = (P_2 + {_1P_2^e})/2 = 102{\cdot}500$.

In year 3 $P_3 = 110{\cdot}250$ so that $_1P_4^e = (P_3 + {_1P_3^e})/2 = 106{\cdot}375$.

In year 4 $P_4 = 115{\cdot}575$ so that $_1P_5^e = (P_4 + {_1P_4^e})/2 = 111{\cdot}975$.

Case B: 'second gear':

In year 1 I_1 and $_2I_1^e = 0$ so that $_2I_2^e = 0$ and
$_2P_2^e = P_1(1 + {_2I_2^e}) = 100$.

In year 2 $I_2 = +5\%$ so that $_2I_3^e = (I_2 + {_2I_2^e})/2 = +2{\cdot}5\%$ and
$_2P_3^e = P_2(1 + {_2I_3^e}) = 107{\cdot}625$.

In year 3 $I_3 = +5\%$ so that $_2I_4^e = (I_3 + {_2I_3^e})/2 = 3{\cdot}75\%$ and
$_2P_4^e = P_3(1 + {_2I_4^e}) = 114{\cdot}384$.

In year 4 $I_4 = +5\%$ so that $_2I_5^e = (I_4 + {_2I_4^e})/2 = 4{\cdot}375\%$
and $_2P_5^e = P_4(1 + {_2I_5^e}) = 120{\cdot}631$.

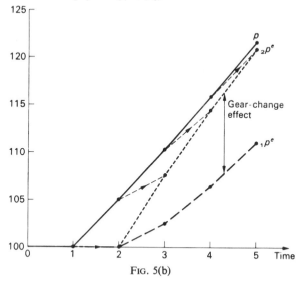

FIG. 5(b)

The actual and expected prices for case B are shown in Figure 5(b). This time the second gear generates the better forecasts which converge on the actual prices while the first-gear forecasts diverge.

While in case B the first-gear expected price level rises by 4·3 per cent between $_1P_4^e$ and $_1P_5^e$ the second-gear expectation rises by 5·3 per cent. This exceeds the actual growth of 5 per cent because it is generated by extrapolating on the basis of rising inflation estimates (3·75, 4·375 per cent) from actual prices which themselves rise by 5 per cent. The real jump, however, occurs if people change gears so that the successive expectations are the first gear expectation of 106·4 for year 4 and the second-gear expectation of 120·7 for year 5. This is an increase of over 13 per cent in the price level expected in successive years as a result of 'catching up' on 5-per-cent inflation!

These examples illustrate a point which is demonstrated formally in the Appendix, namely that the sensitivity of the expected price level to current prices rises as one moves up through the 'gears'. If people are operating in first gear we know that the price expected for next year is a combination of the price previously expected for this year and this year's actual price level; this implies that if this year's actual price is 116 rather than 115 the price now expected for next year will rise by *less* than one point. In second gear, however, the observation of 116 instead of 115 implies a higher observed, and therefore a higher expected, inflation rate which will then be projected on from 116 rather than 115 so that the expected price rises by *more* than one point. Indeed a result of the analysis in the Appendix is that 'second gear' price level expectations are about three times more responsive to current price levels than are 'first gear' expectations, while in 'third gear' the expected price level is about five times as sensitive. This model of changes in expectational 'gear' thus serves to formalize the idea expressed in Chapter III, that the lags in the system—of which the lag of expected prices is very important—are shortened by experience of inflation.

Relation to the Evidence

Apart from its integration of adaptive and rational expectations on the basis of Occam's principle there is some casual empirical evidence for this kind of process[4] in the way the British media publicize official statistics on the price level. They used just to publish the absolute

[4] There is also some statistical evidence for a shift in methods of forecasting in 1967 in a study by Carlson and Parkin based on market-research data. See J. A. Carlson, and J. M. Parkin, 'Inflation Expectations', *Economica*, May 1975, 123–38.

figures and the cumulative decline in the value of money. Then they started to emphasize the excess of each month's figure over the previous year's figure and then the changes in the annual inflation rates implied in the monthly figures.

Rather than construct such a general apparatus, monetarists tend to rely on the apt common sense of the dictum 'you can't fool all the people all the time', but while its long-run implications are clear it is vague (though Abraham Lincoln was not) as to whether you can fool many of them for some of the time. The rational expectations hypothesis is often interpreted as implying that they will *always* be right, subject to unbiased random errors. Our hypothesis is not only consistent with the whole of Lincoln's proposition (which starts 'You *can* fool all the people some of the time') but adds a specification of what they do when they find out.

It would be possible to write out a formula which said that the weights people give to the various possible forecasts depends on the confidence with which they believe they have detected trends of the various orders; this would eliminate the discrete 'gear shift' effect. At the level of the individual this seems too subtle. There is no reason to reject the hypothesis that people use rules of thumb and that these are both fairly simple and liable to discrete changes when they are shown to be misleading. However in the aggregate we might well expect that different people would shift gears at different times so that the aggregate behaviour, if indeed expectations can be aggregated, would be *as if* the composite scheme applied. While this argument would carry a lot of weight in a decentralized competitive economy it is much less persuasive when wage bargaining, in particular, is dominated by relatively few organizations of employees and employers. Moreover the media may well tend to synchronize these shifts of gear independently of the effects of organization such as trade unions, which are the subject of Chapter IX.

The loose theory that there is some systematic relationship between unemployment and inflation which depends on price expectations is not made difficult to test by the fact that the relevant expectations are not directly observable. For if expected prices are assumed to depend on past prices the joint hypothesis is that past prices affect the relationship between unemployment and inflation. Difficulties arise when it comes to testing the stronger theory that price expectations are fully reflected in wage bargains. This hypothesis implies that the expected change in the price level has a coefficient of unity in a regression of wage changes on unemployment. Empirical research in this area involves simultaneous testing of three hypotheses: that unemployment affects wage bargains in a specific way, that expectations are formed in a specific way, and that the two processes interact as hypothesized. Even if the expectations-generating mechanism were fairly stable we are unlikely to model it properly so that the synthesized expectational variable will incorporate errors which bias econometric results. Moreover we have seen that the expectations mechanism is unlikely to be stable, which further undermines the adequacy of existing tests of the relevant hypotheses. These tests[5] have cast doubt on the hypothesis—that expectations are fully reflected in wage bargains—which underlies the theory that inflation would accelerate without limit if an attempt was made to hold it permanently below its normal rate.

An important implication of the accelerationist hypothesis we have formalized here, is that while a little bit of inflation can be used to cover adjustments to various disturbances—by the exploitation of the unresponsiveness of expectations when one starts from price stability—there are very serious risks that 'gear shifts' may take place which would give the process a less stable character. The 'gear shift' hypothesis may also introduce asymmetries between rising and falling expectations would would give them an upward bias as prices decelerate just as they have a downward bias in the early stages of acceleration.

Sources and Further Reading

CAGAN, P., in FRIEDMAN, M., (ed.), *The Monetary Dynamics of Hyperinflation*, 1956.
TURNOVSKY, S. J., 'A Bayesian Approach to the Theory of Expectations', *Journal of Economic Theory*, August, 1969.

[5] See, e.g., R. M. Solow, *Price Expectations and the Behaviour of the Price Level*, Manchester, 1969.

APPENDIX TO CHAPTER VII

As presented in the text the 'adaptive expectations hypothesis' can be expressed in the formula

$$X_t^e = (1-\lambda)X_{t-1}^e + \lambda X_{t-1} \tag{1}$$

where X_t^e is the expectation at time $(t-1)$ of the value the variable X will have taken on at time t, which is written X_t. λ is the weight given to X_{t-1} when forecasting X_t and $(1-\lambda)$ the weight given to the previous forecast (X_{t-1}^e); λ lies between zero and one if both X_{t-1} and X_{t-1}^e contribute to X_t^e.

It is asserted in the text (p. 60) that this method of revising forecasts generates expectations which are weighted averages of past values. This follows from the fact that (1) implies

$$X_{t-1}^e = (1-\lambda)X_{t-2}^e + \lambda X_{t-2}.$$

Substituting this into (1) gives

$$X_t^e = \lambda X_{t-1} + \lambda(1-\lambda)X_{t-2} + (1-\lambda)^2 X_{t-2}^e.$$

Repetition of similar substitution for X_{t-2}^e, X_{t-3}^e etc. yields

$$X_t^e = \lambda[X_{t-1} + (1-\lambda)X_{t-2} + (1-\lambda)^2 X_{t-3} \ldots (1-\lambda)^{n-1} X_{t-n} \ldots] \tag{2}$$

which is clearly a geometrically weighted average of past values of X as the sum of the coefficients $\lambda[1 + (1-\lambda) + (1-\lambda)^2 \ldots]$ is unity.

(1) can also be written as

$$(X_t^e - X_{t-1}^e) = \lambda(X_{t-1} - X_{t-1}^e) \tag{3}$$

which emphasizes the fact that if X is rising steadily X_t^e can only do so if it is consistently smaller than X_t. If X_{t-1}^e is smaller than X_{t-1} in this way X_t^e, which is an average of the two will also be smaller than X_{t-1} as asserted in the text (p. 61).

The 'multi-geared adaptive expectations hypothesis' can be formalized as follows:

If the price *level* P has shown no trend then the relevant first-gear forecast $_1P_t^e$ is given by

whence
$$\left.\begin{aligned} _1P_t^e &= (1-\lambda)_1P_{t-1}^e + \lambda P_{t-1} \\ _1P_t^e &= \lambda P_{t-1} + \lambda(1-\lambda)P_{t-2}\ldots \end{aligned}\right\} \tag{4}$$

where the prefix to P_t^e indicates that this is a first-order forecast. But if there has been a trend in P they will look at the ratio of successive prices $(P_t/P_{t-1})^1$ which is closely related to the rate of inflation

$$I_t = \frac{P_t - P_{t-1}}{P_{t-1}} = \frac{P_t}{P_{t-1}} - 1, \tag{5}$$

and form the second-gear price expectations

where
$$\left.\begin{aligned} _2P_t^e &= P_{t-1}(1+{}_2I_t^e) \\ _2I_t^e &= (1-\mu)_2I_{t-1}^e + \mu I_{t-1} \\ &= \mu I_{t-1} + \mu(1-\mu)I_{t-2}\ldots \end{aligned}\right\} \tag{6}$$

If the rate of inflation I itself reveals a trend, that is, if inflation is accelerating, the forecasts (6) will again consistently underestimate future prices and, on our hypothesis, people will start to forecast prices by the ratio of successive values of the ratio $P_t/P_{t-1} = 1 + I_t$. That is they will work with a measure of the rate of acceleration of inflation (or rather of prices)

$$A_t = \frac{1+I_t}{1+I_{t-1}} = \frac{P_t/P_{t-1}}{P_{t-1}/P_{t-2}} = \frac{P_t\,P_{t-2}}{P_{t-1}^2} \tag{7}$$

and they will form their expectations as

where
$$\left.\begin{aligned} _3P_t^e &= P_{t-1}(1+{}_3I_t^e) \\ (1+{}_3I_t^e) &= (1+I_{t-1})_3A_t^e \\ _3A^e &= (1-\nu)_3A_{t-1}^e + \nu A_{t-1} \\ &= \nu A_{t-1} + \nu(1-\nu)A_{t-2}\ldots \end{aligned}\right\} \tag{8}$$

The 'sensitivity' of P_t^e to P_{t-1} can be measured by the derivative

$\dfrac{\partial P_t^e}{\partial P_{t-1}}$. From (4)

[1] On our earlier argument it might be thought that the *difference* (P_t-P_{t-1}) would be more appropriate than the *ratio* P_t/P_{t-1}. However inflation is a proportionate process, steady inflation is associated with a constant ratio rather than a constant difference. If we were to work with the logarithm of prices the log of the ratio would be the difference of the logs.

$$\frac{\partial_1 P_t^e}{\partial P_{t-1}} = \lambda. \tag{9}$$

From (3) and (6)

$$\begin{aligned}
\frac{\partial_2 P_t^e}{\partial P_{t-1}} &= 1 + {}_2I_t^e + P_{t-1}\frac{\partial_2 I_t^e}{\partial P_{t-1}} \\
&= 1 + {}_2I_t^e + P_{t-1}\mu\frac{\partial I_{t-1}}{\partial P_{t-1}} \\
&= 1 + {}_2I_t^e + \mu\frac{P_{t-1}}{P_{t-2}} \\
&= (1 + I_t^e) + \mu(1 + I_{t-1}).
\end{aligned}$$

Thus if I_{t-1} and ${}_2I_t^e$ are fairly close, as they should be if this is the appropriate level on which to operate, we can write

$$\frac{\partial_2 P_t^e}{\partial P_{t-1}} \approx (1 + \mu)(1 + I). \tag{10}$$

From (5), (6), (7), and (8)

$$\begin{aligned}
\frac{\partial_3 P_t^e}{\partial P_{t-1}} &= (1 + {}_3I_t^e) + P_{t-1}\frac{\partial_3 I_t^e}{\partial P_{t-1}} \\
&= (1 + {}_3I_t^e) + P_{t-1} \cdot {}_3A_t^e\frac{\partial I_{t-1}}{\partial P_{t-1}} + (1 + I_{t-1})P_{t-1}\frac{\partial_3 A_t^e}{\partial P_{t-1}} \\
&= (1 + {}_3I_t^e) + \frac{P_{t-1}}{P_{t-2}} \cdot {}_3A_t^e + (1 + I_{t-1})P_{t-1}\nu\frac{P_{t-3}}{P_{t-2}^2} \\
&= (1 + {}_3I_t^e) + (1 + I_{t-1}) \cdot {}_3A_t^e + (1 + I_{t-1})\nu A_{t-1}.
\end{aligned}$$

If inflation is fairly steady not only will ${}_3I_t^e \approx I_{t-1}$ but ${}_3A_t^e \approx A_{t-1} \approx 1$ so that we can write

$$\frac{\partial_3 P_t^e}{\partial P_{t-1}} \approx (2 + \nu)(1 + I). \tag{11}$$

If $\lambda = \mu = \nu = \frac{1}{2}$ and $I = 10\%$ the three derivatives (9), (10), and (11) take on the values 0·5, 1·65, and 2·75—this is the basis for the factors of 'roughly' three and five referred to in the text (p. 66). If $\lambda = 0·9$, $\mu = \nu = 0·1$, and $I = 10\%$ (9), (10), and (11) take on the values 0·9, 1·21, and 2·31; this case puts lower limits on the factors of $\frac{4}{3}$ and $\frac{5}{2}$. Even without going to the other extreme ($\lambda = 0·1$, $\mu = \nu$ $= 0·9$) $\lambda = \mu = \nu = 0·2$ gives us 0·2, 1·32, and 2·42 for factors of six and 12 respectively (in fact $\lambda = 0·1$, $\mu = \nu = 0·9$ gives factors of twenty and 32!).

VIII THE SHORT-RUN INFLATION/ UNEMPLOYMENT TRADE-OFF AND THE IMPORT OF INFLATION

WE HAVE seen in Chapter VI that when price expectations do not respond immediately to increased monetary demand, monetary expansion will reduce unemployment *temporarily*. This reduction will be associated with a *permanent* rise in the rate of inflation unless unemployment is raised above its normal level at some later date. Thus there are two ways in which we may pay for the temporary reduction of unemployment by inflation. Either we may allow more unemployment later, which will bring the rate of inflation (but not the price level) down again, or we may live with a permanently higher rate of inflation—the costs of which are discussed in Chapters X and XI.

The case in which the short-run trade-off between inflation and unemployment is most likely to make temporary inflation attractive is one in which a policy designed to maintain price stability would lead to swings in the level of unemployment. It may be possible to trade off price stability for employment stability. A policy of consistent monetary expansion at the trend growth rate of output should eliminate any *trend* in prices but does not necessarily lead to the emergence of a *constant* level of unemployment. The levels of recruitment and involuntary separation, resulting from employers' responses to shifts in demand following technological change, and changes in taste, will depend on the rate of those changes, which is not constant. The argument in Chapter III about the economy's tendency to follow a course in a band around its equilibrium path implied that there would be fluctuations in the distance from equilibrium, and in the corresponding level of unemployment, even if there were no forces generating a regular trade cycle.

The conclusion that emerges from combining this proposition with the possibility of a temporary unemployment–inflation trade-off is that inflationary monetary demand increases should be reserved for situations which are both relatively serious in the threatened level of unemployment and either very modest in their inflationary implications or very infrequent. The inflationary implications should be modest so that price expectations are never sensitized by a shift above first gear; the occasions should be infrequent so that if expectations are sensitized time is allowed for desensitization. These requirements may imply that inflation can be used to reduce the costs of adjustment to an outside disturbance only if the disturbance occurs at a time when there has been no recent experience of inflation. In principle the damage done to inflation expectations by one expansionary episode might be compensated by subsequent deflationary policy. However the reluctance of governments to deflate and the asymmetry of the learning process, which would require the deflationary policies to be sustained for most of the time, make this possibility unrealistic.

For these reasons Friedman has advocated rigid adherence to the rule of expanding the money supply at the trend rate of growth of output.[1] A very strong case can be made for relaxing this rule in the case of identifiable discrete disturbances which are known to be infrequent—but in a closed economy such disturbances are likely to be relatively rare. Technological change and changes of taste are seldom general or rapid. This leaves natural disasters, major changes in micro-economic policy (such as the imposition of Selective Employment Tax, Value Added Tax, or other changes in indirect taxes), and possibly disturbances in the labour market resulting from trade-union behaviour (the subject of the next chapter). In fact Friedman's rule itself implies inflation in the face of a natural disaster that reduces output below its trend path. Output will then fall in relation to the money supply so that prices will tend to rise as a result. An inflation of this kind appears to have followed the Black Death which reduced both population and output in Europe in the fourteenth century.

An open economy is, however, more exposed to disturbances; discrete changes in the world prices the country faces, perhaps the result of natural or political disaster elsewhere, are quite possible. The effects of such changes, which have been made topical by the commodity-price boom of 1972 and the oil-price increases of 1973–4, may depend on the exchange-rate regime. For expositional purposes it is easiest to work with flexible exchange rates; this enables us to identify the changes in exchange rates necessary for price-level

[1] See his *A Program for Monetary Stability*, New York, N.Y., 1959.

stability and then to examine the appropriateness of monetary expansion, and the consequent inflation as a response to the problem posed by the relative price change.

Effects on Real Income

A change in a country's terms of trade, the ratio of export to import prices, has two distinct consequences, an effect on its inhabitants' real incomes, and an effect on the equilibrium structure of relative prices and wages, and thus on the allocation of resources within the economy. The consideration of these latter effects can be postponed by taking the example of a country which produces only one good, some of which is exchanged for other goods on world markets. Consider the effects of a rise in the foreign-currency price of the country's imports while the price of its exports, in the same currency, is unchanged. Such a deterioration in the country's terms of trade means that the value of its output on world markets has fallen in relation to the value of the goods it buys, or 'absorbs', for consumption and investment—which, in turn, means that its real expenditures must be cut. If the domestic price level, which reflects the prices of both goods, were maintained this cut in real expenditures would require a cut in money expenditures and money incomes. To maintain the domestic price level the money supply must thus be cut in line with the fall in the country's real income, which is measured by the reduced quantity of the things it uses, for which it could exchange its possibly constant output of the things it produces.

If the domestic price level is to stay unchanged the country's currency must appreciate. If the appreciation is smaller than the increase in the foreign-currency price of imports their domestic price will still rise. Appreciation reduces the price, in domestic currency, of the domestically produced exportable good thus offsetting the effect on the domestic price level of the increase in the domestic price of imports. Suppose the domestic and imported products have equal weights, of one-half, in domestic consumption, or 'absorption'. Then a 10-per-cent increase in the foreign-currency price of all imports would have no effect on the domestic price level if the currency appreciated by 5 per cent. This appreciation would reduce the rise in the domestic price of importables to 5 per cent. The inflationary effect of this increase on the domestic price level would be exactly offset by the 5-per-cent fall in the price of exportables, in terms of domestic currency (we have assumed that the two have equal weight in the price index). The authorities might make the appropriate reduction in the money supply, in which case the currency appreciation should occur automatically under a clean float. Alternatively under a managed system the authorities might raise the exchange rate and would then find that they had to reduce the money supply correspondingly in order to establish payments equilibrium at that rate.

The establishment of this equilibrium is not a simple matter if domestic wages are not flexible in a downward direction. It is important to distinguish three theoretically relevant cases; flexibility of both real and money wages, flexibility of real but not of money wages, and inflexibility of the real wage (in which case there is no question of cutting the money wage). If both real and money wages were flexible, equilibrium would be achieved by both falling by the 5 per cent by which real income has fallen.

If the authorities restrict the money supply, and appreciate the currency, when real, but not money, wages are flexible, domestic producers will find their profit margins squeezed and are likely to respond by cutting employment. The reduction of the real wage to its equilibrium level could, given its flexibility, be achieved by allowing the domestic price level to rise by 5 per cent, and leaving the money supply and exchange rate unchanged. The domestic price of the exportable good and money wages are also unchanged. What falls is the volume of domestic absorption—it falls in line with the fall in real income. In this case inflation is being used to facilitate adjustment to a lower real income; any attempt to 'shield' people from the 'threat' to their living standards, represented by the tendency of the price level to rise relative to domestic wages at the unchanged exchange rate, would add unemployment and a balance-of-payments deficit to the 'imported' inflation.

If the authorities believe that real wages are inflexible, or that it would be very costly in terms of unemployment, social distress, and output foregone to reduce them, they may choose to borrow from abroad, against the security (if any) of the economy's growth prospects, in order to sustain current levels of real absorption. This policy clearly involves a deficit on the current account of the balance of payments. What does it imply for inflation? If no reduction in real wages is planned there is no reason to allow any inflation at all. The problem is then one of maintaining employment despite the fall in the profitability of domestic production at the given level of real wages. This problem could be resolved by a transitional wage subsidy or a cut in pay-roll taxes (such as National Insurance contributions); the consequent government deficit, being the counterpart of the trade deficit, would be financed by foreign borrowing, and would not increase the domestic money supply. Thus in such an economy, with inflexible real wages, the optimal rseponse to a 10-per-cent rise in import prices might consist of a 5-per-cent revaluation of its currency and the introduction of a temporary 5-per-cent wage subsidy to be phased out over two or three years if the underlying growth rate is 2 or 3 per cent per annum. As far as the real-income effect of an adverse change in the terms of trade is concerned, we conclude that unemployment and inflation should be used only to the extent that they would ease any necessary reduction of real wages.

Effects on Resource Allocation in the Multi-Product Case

Let us now turn to the effects on resource allocation. These can be introduced by the removal of the assumption of the previous argument that the country in question produces only one good. Suppose instead that it also produces some goods of the type it imports—an import-competing (importable) good—as well as exportable goods and non-tradables such as retail services, restaurant meals, and construction activity, which together account for one-half of domestic 'absorption'. For simplicity we continue to assume that importables and exportables loom equally large in the country's 'absorption' of goods and services so that a 10-per-cent increase in the foreign-currency price of all imports would still have no effect on the domestic price level if the currency appreciated by 5 per cent.

If this appreciation takes place the situation will differ significantly from the previous case: the production of import-competing goods will have become more profitable than the production of exports. If importables and exportables are equally important in the country's absorption, it is clear that exportables must have the larger share of its output. This implies that the 5-per-cent fall in the domestic price of exportables affects more producers than does the 5-per-cent rise in the price of importables. Sackings, or reduced hirings, by the manufacturers of exportables, whose profits fall, will therefore tend to exceed the extra hirings by producers of importables, whose profits rise. The net effect is that unemployment rises; this reflects the abnormal deviation of the actual distribution of labour, between importable and exportable industries (and related non-tradable activities), from the new equilibrium, and the consequent need for abnormally large shifts of resources.

If the deterioration in the terms of trade came about through a fall in the foreign-currency price of exportables, instead of a rise in the price of importables, domestic-price stability would still require a fall in the money supply, but in this case it would be accompanied by a *devaluation* of the domestic currency. In line with the previous example a 10-per-cent fall in the foreign-currency price of exports would require a 5-per-cent devaluation which would cause a 5-per-cent rise in the domestic price of importables to offset the 5-per-cent net fall in the domestic price of exportables. Once the exchange rate has changed the consequences of the fall in export prices and the rise in import prices are identical; in both cases real incomes fall by the same amount and unemployment will rise as resources shift from the production of exportables to importables.

In the face of this additional transitional unemployment the authorities might well choose to inflate the economy, reducing the money supply by less than the fall in real income, and revaluing by less, or devaluing by more, than the amounts suggested above. At least the smaller revaluation and larger devaluation would be necessary if other countries, which must on average experience an improvement in their terms of trade if ours deteriorate, maintain their domestic-price levels. Might they want to inflate too?

In fact they could well choose to inflate since the same *relative* price change, and the consequent need to shift resources, and hence rising unemployment, affects them as it affects us—although they have no problem of reduced real incomes. If the foreign price of a country's exports rises it must revalue its currency if it wants to preserve its domestic-price level. On the other hand, if its imports fall in price it must devalue. But in both cases the money supply should rise in line with the increase in their real income. In order to facilitate the necessary shift of resources, from the production of their importables to exportables, they might try to exploit people's tendency to think in money terms by a temporary inflation and thus revalue by less, or devalue by more, than otherwise, increasing the money supply more than the increase in real income. In this way variations in relative prices on a world-wide scale may have a world-wide inflationary bias.

Changes in the Terms of Trade and the Causation of Inflation

This analysis raises important questions. Can a government that adopts the policy suggested here in response to a change in its terms of trade be held responsible for the consequent domestic inflation? Could it reasonably claim that the inflation was caused by changes in international prices beyond its control? If we grant this claim we are at least halfway towards the 'cost-push' position that domestic inflation may be the result of external cost pressures independent of monetary factors. Although some of the issues involved may be semantic, or even relate to the ethics of apportioning responsibility, they have attracted considerable attention and are worth analysing.

We saw in Chapter IV that under flexible exchange rates a country should be able to maintain domestic-price stability even though the rest of the world was inflating. We also saw that this was more difficult under the 'adjustable peg' quasi-fixed-rate system. Under the latter system a country's authorities may be able to blame domestic inflation on external events—but only as long as they can justify not floating the currency. Realistically the imported inflation would probably have reached significant proportions before the authorities could screw up the courage to float. All this related to the import of inflation caused by excess monetary expansion in other countries at a time of equilibrium in real magnitudes. What of the terms of trade changes discussed above? Did the 1972 commodity-price boom make some inflation in commodity-importing countries inevitable?

The answer suggested by our analysis is very simple, it is 'No, not inevitable, but possibly wise, if money, but not real wages, were inflexible while price expectations were insensitive.' Where does this answer leave the *causal* status of import-price increases with respect to domestic inflation, which is the issue raised by the 'cost-push' theory? Since many links in economists' 'causal chains' consist of agents' rational, but freely chosen, responses, a commentator must be allowed to say that the import-price rise *caused* the inflation that followed the authorities' response. The authorities themselves, however, cannot make much of this argument since to do so they must deny the conscious wisdom of that response—they cannot claim credit for choosing wisely while denying that they rejected an alternative policy involving more unemployment and *less inflation*. It may, of course, be argued that the choice was forced on the constitutional 'authorities' by other powers, such as trade unions, who would not stand for the unemployment implied by the alternative strategy. It then becomes a moot point, for both the commentator and the constitutional authorities, whether the inflation was caused by the deterioration in the terms of trade or by the political power of the unions.

To say of an inflationary episode in a particular country that its *ultimate* cause was an import-price increase (the *proximate* cause being the authorities' monetary and exchange-rate policy) does not go very far to meet the cost-push position. We have distinguished two reasons for inflating in response to a change in the terms of trade; first, if the change is adverse, and if money, but not real, wages are inflexible, temporary inflation might facilitate the achievement of the new equilibrium real wage. This argument applies not only to the cost-push case of an import-price rise, but equally to an export-price fall. The second reason for inflating was as a response to the problems of reallocating resources after *any* change in the terms of trade. This argument not only applies symmetrically to an import-price rise and an export-price fall, as above, but it would also apply to an export-price rise or even an import-price fall!

Moreover, from a world-wide viewpoint a change in relative prices cannot be regarded as autonomous. The commodity-price boom of 1972 was associated with an exceptional increase in demand by industrialized countries the economies of which all experienced expansive phases simultaneously—and monetary factors played a large part in these expansions. As explained in Chapter III, commodities typically show a quicker price response to increased monetary demand than do industrial products. This is illustrated in Figure 6 which shows (in terms of U.S. dollars) indices of total international reserves of industrial countries, an important element of the world monetary base, the export prices of developed areas, and the Economist index of commodities (excluding oil). International reserves rose by almost 50 per cent in 1971, commodity prices by about 25 per cent in 1972, and developed areas' export prices by the same amount the next year. Part of the deterioration of the terms of trade of industrial countries associated with these changes was thus merely the change in relative prices of raw materials and industrial products characteristic of a particular phase in the inflationary process.

The oil-price increase of 1973–4 does look more like a genuinely autonomous disturbance in international prices, if not actually an act of war, but even this had an inflationary background. Oil prices were

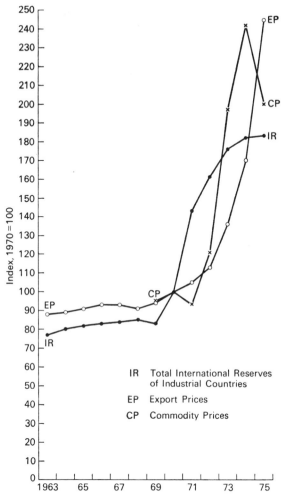

FIG. 6
Sources: International Reserves and Developed Areas Export Prices, *International Financial Statistics.* Commodity Prices, *Bank of England Quarterly Bulletin,* September 1975.

fixed in U.S. dollars, as inflation in the U.S. accelerated, and the U.S. dollar depreciated in relation to other currencies, so the amount of manufactured imports the oil exporters could buy with their oil production diminished. On this view the Arab-Israeli war was merely the catalyst which precipitated the crystallization of, and reaction to, the growing discontent of the producers at the erosion of their position by inflation in the industrial West.

Sources and Further Reading.   As for Chapter IV.

IX TRADE UNIONS AND INFLATION

THE ARGUMENT of the previous chapter that discrete changes in import prices might justify temporary inflation, though developed from a background of 'monetarist' analysis, involved conceding that 'cost-push' theories contained at least a germ of truth. Their proponents typically lay more stress on the activities of trade unions, which are the subject of this chapter, than on the changes in the cost of imported goods. In this Chapter we shall discuss the possibility that autonomous disturbances originating in the domestic labour market have effects analogous to the international disturbances just considered. But first we re-examine those points in the argument so far, an argument based on fundamentally competitive assumptions, which require modification in the light of the existence of monopolistic trade unions.

Unions and Labour-Market Equilibria

The formal analysis underlying the arguments of Chapters I–VI is seriously undermined by the existence of trade-union and producer monopolies since the general equilibrium analysis on which it rests has only been carried out rigorously for the competitive case. Proofs of the existence, uniqueness, and stability of competitive equilibrium are difficult; for the general non-competitive case they do not exist.[1] This does not mean that the previous analysis is irrelevant, any more than it would have been irrelevant in a competitive economy before rigorous proofs for that case became available,[2] but that we do not have strong *theoretical* grounds for believing it is relevant.

Even if this objection is not fatal to their position monetarists do recognize that the pattern of trade-union organization and monopoly power will influence the equilibrium pattern of real wages and the

[1] See, e.g., K. J. Arrow, and F. H. Hahn, *General Competetive Anaylsis*, San Francisco, California, 1971.
[2] Between 1930 and 1955.

equilibrium allocation of labour. This implies that *changes* in the pattern of union power have to be added to the changes in tastes and technology generating the movements which, in the presence of friction, create frictional unemployment. Unions tend to reduce wage flexibility and thus to shift the burden of adjustment to all changes from prices and wages to quantities and employment. This change is one of degree rather than kind since, as we argued in Chapter V, some wage rigidity, and the consequent reliance on employment adjustment, would characterize competitive capital intensive industries.

In these two ways unions tend to raise the normal/natural level of unemployment; it can, however, be argued that their activities also have the opposite effect (probably incidentally) by increasing the efficiency of job search in two ways. By collective bargaining they establish uniform wage structures for relatively large categories of jobs. If people bargained individually one could find out what one would earn in a given job only by trying to negotiate a rate for it. Thanks to the activities of unions the employers' opportunities to discriminate are substantially reduced and the amount of search required falls proportionately. Secondly by informing their members of the results of their central research on pay in other sectors, on which they may base a wage claim, they disseminate information more widely and cheaply than would the unaided grapevine.

These arguments all relate to effects of trade unions which are essentially independent of inflation, although anything that raises the normal/natural rate of unemployment is liable to generate demands for policies with inflationary effects. Trade unions may also tend to destabilize the system by contributing to the synchronization of changes of expectational 'gear', and the rapid adoption of the revised expectations as the basis for collective bargaining. Indeed the role of professionals and research departments in collective bargaining suggests that the strong form of the rational expectations hypothesis, in which expectations are derived from the application of appropriate theories, may become relevant. This would all but eliminate the lags inherent in adaptive behaviour—however it is doubtful whether the theory set out in this book is widely held even in the research departments of British unions.

Unions in the Inflationary Process

In the presence of trade unions we also have to rewrite the section of the 'story' in Chapter VI that referred to employers raising wages in the course of a monetary expansion in order to maintain an appropriate flow of job-applicants. This argument cannot apply to an employer who has conceded higher wages than he would otherwise have done as a result of trade-union pressure. An effect of trade-union monopolies is so to distort relative wages that there is an excess supply of labour to those industries and skills whose wages they have raised. However not all trades are unionized and wage increases in response to increased demand are likely, on the arguments of Chapter VI, to occur in the less-organized sectors first if price increases do not lead wage rises, i.e. if inflation does not reduce real wages. If, on the other hand, inflation does reduce real wages, as in the first 'story' of Chapter VI, it is the organized sectors in which the wage response is likely to be most prompt.

When unions negotiate on the basis of maintaining their members' real incomes—and this becomes relevant at some stage whatever the initial response—the system of progressive taxation is liable to lead some unions to make demands which appear to be very high in relation to the recent inflation, and thus to aggravate any tendency towards acceleration. This is because the maintenance of living standards requires that the *post-tax* wage keep pace with prices: suppose prices rise by 10 per cent, a 10-per-cent wage increase will be taxed at the worker's *marginal* rate of tax, about 30 per cent, to the extent that his *average* rate of tax is less than 30 per cent a 10-per-cent increase in his pre-tax wage will raise his post-tax income by less than 10 per cent. More precisely it is shown in footnote 3 below that to maintain the workers' living standard wages must rise by the rate of inflation times $(1 - a/1 - m)$—where a is the average and m the marginal rate of tax.[3] At the tax threshold $a = 0$ and if $m = 33\frac{1}{3}$ per cent

[3] Post-tax, or disposable, income

$$D = Y - T$$

where Y is pre-tax income and T, tax paid, is a function of income $T(Y)$. Then

$$\frac{dD}{dY} = 1 - \frac{dT}{dY} \equiv 1 - m$$

while

$$\frac{D}{Y} = 1 - \frac{T}{Y} = 1 - a.$$

Thus the elasticity of disposable income with respect to pre-tax income

$$\frac{Y}{D}\frac{dD}{dY} = \frac{1 - m}{1 - a}$$

and $\left(\dfrac{1 - a}{1 - m}\right)$ is the percentage by which Y must rise if D is to rise by 1 per cent.

(or $\frac{1}{3}$) the factor $\dfrac{1-a}{1-m} = 1\frac{1}{2}$; inflation at 10 per cent would require the wages of those on the tax threshold to rise by 15 per cent if they were to maintain their real net incomes.

If the tax threshold (or exemption level) were indexed, or if marginal tax rates were lower in the region of the threshold, the problem might be less acute. However the type of indexation required is difficult to reconcile with annual budgets and annual wage increases which are not in step. Annual adjustment would leave the previous argument unaffected if workers compare their net income the week after the rise with the week before rather than a year before when the exemption level was lower in money terms. Until 1970 there were 'reduced rates' of tax on incomes just over the exemption level; these were abolished because, when combined with rough indexation of the threshold, their administrative cost became excessive under inflation even at fairly modest rates. Inflation each year took many people just over the exemption level; dossiers had to be built up on the basis of which their liability on a little income to a low rate of tax was established; before any significant revenue had been collected from them the exemption level was raised again and they ceased to be taxpayers. This is a good example of the way in which inflation raises the costs of institutional arrangements which might reduce inflationary pressures.

In Chapter VI it was argued that the 'story' according to which inflation reduced real wages was probably oversimplified. The effects of trade unions on the alternative 'story', as described above, suggest the following theoretical account of the place of trade unions in the inflationary process which amplifies the sketchy statement in Chapter III. An expansion of monetary demand, which might be based on a 'dash for growth', or be a response to changed terms of trade, leads to a relatively rapid rise in the wages of the unorganized workers in the growth sectors of the economy. As time passes the unions discover that they have slipped behind and succeed in enforcing parity. This leaves the unorganized workers in the declining sectors with substantially lower relative real wages. Some of the union-negotiated wage increases may have been obtained by strikes in essential services with attendant publicity. A natural reaction of the unorganized is to join unions and this further changes the pattern of labour-market monopolies and the equilibrium structure of real wages and the natural rate of unemployment (at least temporarily).

Autonomous Wage Push?

This account attributes no role to *autonomous* labour-market disturbances which, as was noted above, are central to a 'cost-push' theory of inflation. The logical possibility of such a disturbance cannot be denied; if ten million workers suddenly banded together and demand that their money wage be doubled, their employers and the authorities would be in real difficulties and temporary inflation might well ensue. The reasons for regarding this possibility as of doubtful relevance are threefold.

First the demand for higher *money* wages is an odd, indeed an irrational, demand; if all the unions want is money they can be given more together with inflation which will restore the initial situation in real terms. If what they want is higher *real* wages then the co-ordinators of a mass demand should recognize the constraint of available resources. Income from employment and self-employment has accounted for over 80 per cent of National Income in recent years. Secondly, and more importantly, it is difficult to reconcile such behaviour with the rationality of those concerned, not because the demands are not in their interest, but because the rational pursuit of self-interest leads to discontinuities in behaviour only when circumstances, or perception of circumstances, change discretely. Finally most of the instances of allegedly spontaneous upsurges of union militancy can be fitted quite easily into the theoretical account just given, in which unions appeared as responding to, rather than being responsible for, inflation.

The second argument can easily be overstated. This argument from the consistent behaviour of rational agents has three weaknesses: it overlooks all the well-known problems of forming a rational collective from rational individuals.[4] Secondly 'consistency' may apply either at a point in time—in which case it is an aspect of rationality—or over time in which case it refers to the stability of preferences, possibly under the influence of habit. While individuals may be fairly consistent in both senses a smooth trend of individual preferences from preference for one faction to preference for another with a very

---

[4] See, e.g., M. Olson, *The Logic of Collective Action*, Cambridge, Mass., 1965.

different policy may lead to a discontinuity in the leadership which may determine union policy. Thirdly even if unions were rational and neither the fickleness of fashionable ideology nor the power of individual, but changing, leaders had any effect, there would still be problems associated with inevitable ignorance.

Monetarists sometimes argue that unions are just like other monopolists and maximize a stable objective function subject to certain market-imposed constraints. What matters, however, is their perception of those constraints. What happens if the union leaders do not know how many of their members will lose their jobs for each pound by which they raise the real wage? Other monopolists conduct market research, but that is difficult when one is confronting one's customers across the bargaining table. In this state of ignorance it is difficult to rule out a union deciding, as evidence accumulates, that it has got the demand elasticity wrong, and that to buy a lot of information by making a big change is appropriate. Thus big changes in relative real wages cannot be ruled out on theoretical grounds, even if one accepts a crude theory about collective rationality. On the other hand whether such autonomous changes would occur on a sufficient scale to have a noticeable impact on macro-economic variables is very doubtful.

The evidence to the contrary to which British cost-push theorists most frequently point are the major industrial confrontations and strikes, the occurrence of which was not entirely predictable, and the consequences of which certainly appear to have been widespread imitation and accelerating inflation. To reconcile those in which substantial changes in relative real wages have indeed occurred with the account given above one should notice three things about them. The best-publicized strikes, which have been in the public sector, have taken place when the inflationary process had already acquired considerable momentum but no inflationary equilibrium had been established. Secondly they were fought specifically on the basis that public-sector wages had been slipping behind those paid elsewhere, and these claims were substantiated. Thirdly, and most importantly, in several cases (miners and nurses for example, although the first case might have been influenced by increased government 'protection' for the domestic coal industry) they were followed by increased recruitment rather than the cut-back which would follow a real-wage-raising initiative of the type associated with the fuller exertion of monopoly power.

If this impressionistic account is correct it implies that the monetarists are right when they say that 'fundamentally' the source of inflation is excess monetary demand at some time possibly long past or even far away. However it also implies that the role of the unions is considerably greater than their static monopoly theory would suggest. Unions may be sluggish in responding to changed conditions, they may suddenly 'wake up' and become 'militant', their expectations will change 'gear' and their doing so will have effects which will probably lead the authorities to inflate. But none of these events is likely to be truly independent of the previous history of the inflationary process and this entitles the monetarists to question their 'causal' status. On the other hand these arguments do suggest that inflation might well accelerate temporarily although unemployment was above the trend level of its 'natural' or 'normal' rate; this might be described—though it is not clear that the description is very helpful —by saying that the 'normal rate of unemployment' is subject to discrete changes in the course of the inflationary process of a kind very different from the trends to which reference was made at the end of Chapter V.

Sources and Further Reading

BALOGH, T., *Labour and Inflation*, London, 1970.

CODDINGTON, A., *Theories of the Bargaining Process*, London, 1968.

DE MENIL, G., *Bargaining: Monopoly Power versus Union Power*, Cambridge, Mass., 1971.

HABERLER, G., PARKIN, J. M., and SMITH, H, *Inflation and the Unions*, London, 1972.

HOLT, C., in PHELPS, *et. al.*, op. cit. (see Chapter V).

JACKSON, D., TURNER, H. A., and WILKINSON, F., *Do Trade Unions Cause Inflation?*, Cambridge, 1972.

JONES, A., *The New Inflation: The Politics of Prices and Incomes*, London, 1972.

PITCHFORD, J. D., *A Study of Cost and Demand Inflation*, Amsterdam, 1963.

PURDY, D. L., and ZIS, G., in LAIDLER and PURDY, (eds.), op. cit.

X THE COSTS OF ANTICIPATED INFLATION

MOST PEOPLE think that inflation is a bad thing for very bad reasons. In this chapter we examine some of the effects of inflation such as making it easier for the government to raise taxes and redistributing the burden of taxes from labour to property income. These changes can be criticized either in themselves or because they ought only to be introduced by the government after proper debate and legislation. However one would not expect much more than half the population to disapprove of such changes on other than procedural grounds. Another effect of inflation is to raise the real cost of the services of cash holdings and bank accounts, but this is not what many people have in mind[1] and is in any case largely offset at low levels of inflation by the government's revenue from printing the inflationary increases in the money supply which enables them to provide more services for given taxes. The serious costs of inflation are associated with the consequences of the uncertainty it generates and the analysis of these is quite a technical matter, as we shall see in the next chapter.

Why, if inflation does not have obvious costs, are people so nearly unanimous in condemning it? There seem to be three plausible reasons. Inflation is often associated with attempts to reduce real disposable incomes, whether as an alternative to taxation to finance a war, or as a response to the deterioration in a country's terms of trade. In both cases inflation is merely incidental to a downward adjustment in real income—but much of the odium of the latter may attach itself to the former.

The second reason is that even when a person's real income is rising he is liable to feel that inflation is making him poorer. This in turn is the result of two effects. The first is that inflation makes the price level an issue: if people take the price level as given then being better

[1] J. Tobin, 'Inflation and Unemployment', *American Economic Review*, 1972, p. 16.

off means having more money and vice versa. More generally, being better off means *either* having more money *or* facing lower prices, and it is easier to resent the level of prices if they have just risen, especially if they have risen by more than you expected when you got your last pay rise. This brings us to the second aspect: suppose there is 10-per-cent inflation and someone gets annual increases of 15 per cent; clearly the trend of his real income is upwards at 5 per cent p.a. Yet on 364 days out of 365 he is poorer than the day before.

A third possibility relates to the effect of inflation inside the household: one of the least-studied economic bargains is that struck between husbands and wives; if this bargain is surrounded by any inhibition or embarrassment inflation will tend to generate tension within the family. If wives do not know how fast their husbands' wages are rising, while husbands do not know how prices are rising, it is possible that wives react to a 10-per-cent rise in prices by, say, cutting real purchases by 5 per cent and asking for a 5-per-cent increase in their housekeeping. If the husband's net income has in fact risen by 10 per cent he will resent the reduced quality of the meals his wife provides while she resents the reduced real value of her housekeeping.

All of this is mere conjecture, designed to explain the general agreement that inflation is bad when conventional economic analysis, which tends to overlook the uncertainty considered in the next chapter, has failed to produce many generally persuasive arguments. To this conventional analysis we now turn.

The effects of inflation can be analysed in several different ways, of which the simplest is the analysis of confidently and correctly anticipated inflation. If inflation is incorrectly anticipated people will discover that they have made mistakes and there may be costs associated with these mistakes although there is an unexpected winner for each unexpected loser if everyone had the same (wrong) expectations. Whether or not inflation is expected people may be uncertain about future price levels and this uncertainty has a cost which is a cost of inflation to the extent that inflation increases the uncertainty. Each of these effects of inflation is considered in turn, taking as our reference point an economy in which the price level is maintained and expected to be maintained perfectly constant.

If inflation were perfectly anticipated its effects could be reduced to a low level. Suppose we knew that prices would rise by 10 per cent a year then this inflation would have virtually no effect if all contracts previously made in money terms were interpreted in terms of money adjusted by the appropriate compound-interest factor. The same would apply with only slightly more complexity if the perfectly anticipated inflation was not constant. For reasons which will become apparent later it is preferable not to call this adjustment 'indexation' but 'escalation'. If *all* contracts, explicit and implicit, were escalated by the known rate of inflation, inflation would have no effects and no costs.

Such complete escalation requires that interest at the rate of inflation be paid not only on bank deposits but also to holders of normally non-interest-bearing government debt such as notes and coins. The payment of this interest at the rate of inflation on the high-powered money supply, if paid by the creation of money, implies that the quantities of high-powered and broad money both grow at the rate of inflation which is therefore sustainable. Other interest rates would, in effective nominal terms, also rise by 10 per cent. Since dividends are not contractual the escalation procedure is inapplicable; however if both company accounts and the tax system were properly adjusted, unchanged real dividends would presumably be paid. Thus the costs of perfectly anticipated inflation arise from the failure fully to implement the escalation procedure, of which the outstanding failures are the payment of interest on legal tender and the adjustment of the tax system: from these arise most of the other distortions.

Inflation as a Tax on Liquid Assets

Consider first an inflationary economy with inflation-proof taxes but no interest payments on legal tender: inflation then raises the real cost of holding legal tender; if banks were allowed to pay interest on chequing accounts competitive pressure would force them to do so and people might stop using cash altogether. However there would still be two costs; one is the cost of writing a cheque and waiting for other people to write cheques each time you get on a bus. The second is that even the cost of holding a chequing account at the bank will have increased; this is because the banks will not be able to pay an interest rate equal to the rate of inflation as long as they are required to hold any of their assets in the form of legal tender. If 10 per cent of deposits are matched by legal tender, and the nominal (money) returns on all other assets rise by 10 per cent, the banks' total receipts rise by only 9 per cent. If the real wages of bank employees and the banks' real profits are to be unchanged only 9 per cent can be paid on deposits although 10 per cent is needed to offset inflation.

Thus the real costs of holding money in the bank rises, though by much less than the cost of holding legal tender. This is equivalent to a rise in the price of the services obtained by holders of these assets whose welfare falls accordingly. However that is not quite the end of the matter: we noted above that payment of interest on legal tender at the inflation rate would absorb the government's proceeds from operating the printing presses at the rate required to maintain the inflation. If such interest is not paid these proceeds are free in the hands of the authorities and can be distributed, say as a uniform payment per head to every member of the society. In this case would the typical person's welfare still fall?

The answer is uncertain: the raised cost of holding money when interest is not paid at the rate of inflation reduces the demand for real money balances. Ten per cent of the reduced real balances is less than 10 per cent of the original quantity, which is the sum required to compensate people for the ravages of inflation. This suggests that the typical person's welfare would fall, but the argument is not conclusive; in the example given the proceeds of the money issue are distributed uniformly to everyone, which means that there is net redistribution from large holders of money (probably the rich) to small holders of money (probably the poor). Inflation is indeed a tax and shares with nearly all taxes this characteristic that the cash value of the costs they impose on the payers exceed the revenue received by the government. This excess is known as the 'deadweight' burden of the tax and can be illustrated by reference to the income tax; suppose that a proportionate income tax at $33\frac{1}{3}$ per cent on a man earning £1 an hour induces him to cut his working hours from forty to thirty-nine while leaving the pre-tax wage itself unchanged. The man actually pays tax of £13 to the government but he is also induced to spend an extra hour of 'leisure' and to reduce his expenditure by £14, not £13; depending on the value to him of this hour of 'leisure' the deadweight burden is some fraction of this extra pound. The redistribution brought about by the inflation tax may enable the authorities to achieve their objectives with, say, a lower income-tax rate and that involves *reducing* the deadweight burden of that tax which may more than offset the deadweight cost of the inflation 'tax'.

Thus the question can be, and has been, asked in the following terms.[2] Inflation has some effects similar to a tax on money holdings: what is the optimal rate for such a tax? There is now a growing literature on optimal commodity taxation[3] which reinforces the traditional proposition that the deadweight burden of a commodity tax is low if the demand-and-supply elasticities of the commodity are low. In fact the marginal cost of raising revenue by taxing any one commodity varies with both the elasticities and the level of the tax. The deadweight loss from the first pound of revenue collected on any one commodity considered in isolation is always negligible, and where other commodities are already taxed the 'deadweight burden' may actually be a gain. Thus a shift from explicit commodity taxation to the taxation of money holdings through inflation, probably reduces the over-all welfare costs of revenue at very low rates of inflation; how low is low for these purposes depends on the amount of revenue to be raised and all the elasticities.

Whatever the revenue required there is a maximum contribution that can be extracted from money holders. Just as the tax on whisky could be raised to a level at which demand fell so heavily that revenue fell, so could the inflation tax become self-defeating as a revenue raiser, in which case the deadweight burden is borne to no avail. Thus these costs are clearly relevant and possibly substantial under hyperinflation, when a real flight from money takes place, but the situation is much less clear at more modest rates of inflation. Further complications arise in a growing economy in which the authorities can increase the money supply without causing inflation; if inflation reduces the ratio of real balances to income it reduces the revenue available from this source. Moreover the loss of revenue requires the authorities to issue interest-bearing debt, the servicing of which imposes further revenue requirements.

Inflation and Personal Taxation

The same ambiguity surrounds the consequences of failure to adjust the income-tax system. Broadly the consequences are that effective tax rates rise and the burden of taxation is shifted from

---

[2] e.g. by E. S. Phelps, 'Inflation in a Theory of Public Finance', *Swedish Journal of Economics*, 1973.

[3] e.g. P. A. Diamond, and J. A. Mirrlees, 'Optimal Taxation and Public Production', *American Economic Review*, 1971.

labour to capital. Whether these are good or bad changes depends on whether the initial arrangements were optimal or not—a subject on which unanimity is unlikely: here we deal only with the mechanics of these effects. In fact the first is so obvious that it need not detain us long. If there is an exemption level (personal allowance) and the tax rate thereafter is constant over quite a long range (as it is in Britain) then a typical man's average tax rate is the constant rate times the ratio of taxable income (income in excess of the exemption level) to total income. If the exemption level is fixed in money terms inflation raises this ratio. Consider a man with an income of £2,000 and an exemption level of £1,000 in which case his average rate is half the marginal rate. If inflation at 10 per cent p.a. for a five-year period raises his income to over £3,000 while the exemption level is unchanged, his average rate rises to two-thirds of the marginal rate.

This effect, and that by which inflation lowers the real income at which higher marginal rates are applied, is in practice largely offset by periodic revisions of the exemption level and other points in the tax structure. However if such revisions cannot be reliably anticipated people may behave as though the tax on their earnings was raised by inflation, a result which has effects mentioned in Chapter IX. Moreover, such revisions do not deal with the increased tax burden on investment income under inflation; consider, for instance, the tax implications of the need to pay interest on money under a balanced inflation. Under most tax codes this would be treated as taxable income: if there were 10-per-cent inflation and 10-per-cent interest were paid on money the interest would be taxable, say at 50 per cent. In this case the net return to holding money would be $+5$ per cent in money terms but -5 per cent in real terms although the same tax code allowed people a zero real return on their money after tax in the absence of inflation.

Indeed if all interest rates rose by 10 percentage points, so that bank deposits previously paying 5 per cent now paid 15 per cent, the net nominal return, after tax at 50 per cent, would rise from $2\frac{1}{2}$ to $7\frac{1}{2}$ per cent: the after-tax real return would have fallen from $+2\frac{1}{2}$ to $-2\frac{1}{2}$ per cent. Thus any form of fixed interest investment is effectively subjected to an annual wealth tax at a rate equal to the rate of inflation times the marginal income-tax rate ($\frac{10}{100} \times \frac{50}{100} = 5$ per cent).

This effect might not apply if bonds paid out the same real income as in the absence of inflation and compensated for the effects of inflation by raising the nominal redemption value. This is effectively what should happen to equities under balanced inflation—dividends and share prices would rise in step with the price level. Unfortunately, however, the increase in the share price would be taxed as a capital gain in many countries (including Britain) even if the share price had done no more than match the rise in the general price level. Thus a balanced inflation, with all other payments escalated, involves an increased burden of taxation on property income relative to that on labour income if both are subject to conventional income and capital-gains taxes.[4] The increase would be by an amount equal to the rate of inflation times something between the rate of income tax and the effective capital-gains tax rate. The nominal capital-gains tax rate is lower than the income-tax rate in most countries and the effective rate is even lower as the tax is usually imposed only on realizations and can thus be postponed. Because the inflation adjustment on interest payments is taxed more heavily than that on dividends and share values such an economy would be distorted in the direction of those activities financed by equity capital rather than by debt capital.

Inflation and Company Taxation

This argument is weakened in its application to Britain by the fact that companies receive tax relief on both their investment and their interest payments, but it is noteworthy that much of the value of the latter relief might be lost were company-profits taxation fully adjusted for the impact of inflation on companies. To date more progress has been made in inflation-proofing company tax than in adjusting personal taxation; the preceding argument shows what dangers might arise if the two are not considered together.[5] Changes are necessary in company taxation because in the absence of special measures conventional company taxation imposes an increasing burden under inflation in three distinct ways: through the taxation of capital gains and in the two areas in which tax-deductible costs have to be spread over time, i.e. fixed and working capital.

[4] There are other taxes which are less difficult to adjust to inflation—e.g. an expenditure tax or a wealth tax. A comprehensive income tax which taxed the sum of consumption and the change in *real* wealth (i.e. the money change minus the inflation rate times initial wealth) is also relatively easy to adjust. See P. A. Diamond, 'Inflation and the Comprehensive Income Tax Base', *Journal of Public Economics*, August 1975.

[5] See paragraph 689 of the Sandilands report, op. cit.

In the case of fixed capital the standard accounting procedure is to treat as a cost a certain fraction (say $1/n$th) of the cost of acquiring an asset in each of the subsequent n years. Escalation requires that this depreciation charge should rise in line with the rate of inflation. This might also coincide with the replacement cost of the asset but if relative prices were liable to change in the absence of inflation replacement-cost depreciation and escalation for inflation are not equivalent. Tax codes tend to allow only historic cost depreciation as a deductible expense in which case company taxation adds to inflationary distortions. There has, however, been a tendency in several countries to introduce and extend 'accelerated depreciation' in parallel with, but not explicitly on account of, accelerating inflation. Under accelerated depreciation one might be allowed to treat $2/n$th of the cost of a machine as a deductible cost in each of the subsequent $n/2$ years even though the machine's useful life was n years. This tends to lower the company's tax burden in the early years and raise it by the same money amount in later years. With a positive nominal-interest rate, that is positive in money terms, this postponement of tax liability is of positive value to the firm.

The extreme case of accelerated depreciation is the 100-per-cent first year allowance ('free depreciation') when the whole cost of a machine is treated as a deductible expense in the year it is incurred. Under this system historic and replacement costs are equal in the year the tax allowance is claimed, which is the year in which the machine is bought. Thus no distortion arises from inflation provided that firms always have sufficient profits against which to set their claimed deductions. In practice this is by no means always true and the failure to pay any interest on money claims against the Revenue which are carried forward, means that inflation is liable to reduce the real value of money tax allowances.

As far as working capital is concerned, the system effective in Britain until 1974 was to allow the cost of materials as a deductible expense only when the products made from them were eventually sold. This had the result that inflation added to taxable profits an amount equal to the change in the value of work in progress, if the product price actually charged kept pace with input costs. Suppose that materials and labour costing £100 in one month produce a product selling, in the absence of inflation, for £110 the next month. If inflation takes place at 1 per cent a month the product has to sell for

£111 if pre-tax real rates of profit are to be maintained. But only the £100 is allowed as a cost so that taxable profits are £11. At a 50-per-cent tax rate the net profit rises from £5 to £5·50 and the net nominal rate of return from 5 to 5·5 per cent per month. With inflation at 1 per cent a month the net real return has actually fallen from 5 to 4·5 per cent a month. Both these deficiencies of the company-tax system tend to reinforce the effect of inflation to shift the distribution of income away from capital with possible effects on saving, accumulation, and growth.

So far we have considered only the consequences of the authorities failing to escalate the things for which they are responsible, namely the return on money and the tax system. One would expect considerable pressure for private contracts to escalate under perfectly anticipated inflation but there are at least three serious problems. It was mentioned above that if there were inflation at 10 per cent, 'effective nominal rates of interest' should rise by the same amount—in the absence of an income tax. The reason for this clumsy expression is that if one simply raises the nominal rate on, say, mortgages, by 10 per cent the relevant payments do not escalate.

Problems of High Nominal Interest Rates

Mortgages are calculated on an annuity formula which gives, for the term of the loan, the annual payment which has a present value, discounted at the interest rate, equal to the sum borrowed. If the formula used assumes that the same *money* amount is paid each year then raising the interest rate in step with inflation does not leave things unchanged in real terms. This follows at once from the fact that the uniform money payments will, under inflation, be declining real payments. If the *average* real payment is to be unchanged by inflation, as it must be if the real interest rate is unchanged, then the initial real payments must be higher under inflation. This may create very serious problems for young borrowers who face the heaviest real payments at a time when their ability to pay may not be at a maximum.

This problem could be met in either of two ways, one is for the borrower to borrow more each year—after all, the money value of his house is rising so the collateral is there, and the money value of his income is also rising. However the costs of negotiating the successive loans would be very high unless it were done routinely by the lender in which case it is equivalent to the second solution. This is that the repayment schedule should provide for escalating nominal repayments, the real payments being held constant. This too has its costs since at present there exists no standard procedure for instructing banks to make regularly escalating payments.

There is nothing special about mortgages; the same problem, that under inflation uniform money payments imply declining real payments, applies to all fixed-interest borrowing such as the debentures which finance much industrial investment. Indeed this has been an important contributory cause of the recent cash-flow problem of many firms. However, in this case the possibility of further borrowing is more relevant but the terms on which further loans may be available are uncertain. The perfect anticipation of inflation here postulated does not imply perfect anticipation of changes in *real* interest rates. Forcing firms to borrow for what are, in effect, shorter periods, forces them to take risks they can normally avoid (see further Chapter XI below). Another practical problem, even when inflation is perfectly anticipated, is that as nominal interest rates rise so the timing of transactions becomes more important; this may lead to confusion, inconvenience, and ill temper. Suppose one does not have the right change; if inflation is at 10 per cent a week one cannot say 'Keep it, I'll take it next time' unless one adds 'I'll take 11 pence next week for the 10 you owe me now.' Similarly if one returns goods to a shop and the price has risen in the meantime one should recover more than the initial price. Yet to present this correctly in his accounts the shopkeeper has to treat the two transactions as a loan; he has borrowed money for a few days at the rate of inflation. When shopkeepers' real net margins are less than 5 per cent they can barely afford to run a system even of monthly accounts if inflation is at 1 per cent a month. Customers could effectively get a 1-per-cent discount by buying at the beginning of the month, thus reducing the shop's real profit by 25 per cent. These difficulties, like the cost of re-pricing all the goods on the shelf, and adapting vending machines, arise even if inflation is perfectly anticipated though they are unlikely to be severe if inflation is at less than 10 per cent p.a. The more interesting problems with private contracts are associated with the lack of confidence with which people forecast the rate of inflation. This could be important even if the expected rate of inflation was fairly low.

Sources and Further Reading

BEHREND, H., 'Price and Incomes Images and Inflation', *Scottish Journal of Political Economy*, 1964.

CARSBERG, B. V., HOPE, A. J. B., and SCAPENS, R. W., (eds.), *Studies in Accounting for Inflation*, Manchester, 1976.

LIESNER, T., and KING, M. A., (eds.), *Indexing for Inflation*, London, 1975.

XI THE EFFECTS OF UNANTICIPATED INFLATION: UNCERTAINTY AND INDEXATION

IN THE last chapter we saw that the costs of anticipated inflation at a modest rate might well be quite small. But now we must consider the much more serious costs of *un*anticipated inflation. Unanticipated inflation, and the associated uncertainty about the future level of prices, have effects which are of an entirely different kind and are almost certainly very much greater than those of anticipated inflation. They are approached in this chapter in two ways: we first consider the consequences for an economy that has previously enjoyed price stability of an unexpected, one-for-all, change to inflation at 10 per cent a year. We then discuss the effects of price-level uncertainty, an uncertainty which would be associated with the experience of unexpected, or wrongly predicted, price increases.

An Unexpected Change in the Rate of Inflation

In fact the sudden change in the inflation rate from zero to 10 per cent is not easy to achieve. If the authorities start to inflate the money supply by 10 per cent p.a., prices will not immediately respond. When they do respond the inflation rate will rise, temporarily, to over 10 per cent as the expectation of inflation, and rising nominal interest rates, reduce the demand for real balances. Suppose, however, that the authorities can pursue a money-supply path which does generate a step change in the inflation rate. What will be the transitional consequences for such variables as real wages, unemployment, interest rates, and the distribution of income and wealth?

We have already discussed at length the reasons why unexpected inflation should reduce unemployment, and as the 10-per-cent inflation becomes expected unemployment will tend to return to its normal level although it may have to exceed it if the real wage rises too high in the early stages of the transition. It is somewhat paradoxical that unexpected inflation should raise both employment and real wages; if one believes in diminishing returns the rise in employment should reduce the marginal product and real wage of labour. It is however possible, as noted in Chapter VI, that firms will be misled by their conventional accounts, when the inflation starts, into thinking that their profits are higher than they really are. If this accounting illusion induces them to adopt a pricing policy which implies a fall in real profits, then with rising employment real labour income must also rise.

Another reason why firms might allow real wages to rise is that, as the inflation progresses, they could maintain both their real-dividend and real-investment programmes with lower real profits if they had borrowed money for long periods at the pre-inflationary interest rate. The interest due on these old debts is, like their redemption value, fixed in money terms. Inflation therefore causes it to diminish in real terms, so leaving more room for other claims on real output. Neither of these explanations of why real wages increase at the beginning of an inflation depends at all on the cost-push notion that unions push up money wages and prices follow with a lag.

The impact of the inflation on interest rates and asset prices is one of the more difficult areas because the empirical evidence suggests a slower response here than elsewhere to the adaptation of expectations to the inflation rate. However, the general tendency must be for nominal-interest rates to rise, but in the course of their slow adjustment to a step change in the inflation rate real interest rates will first fall. The rise in nominal rates reduces the money value of old debt, the holders of which experience a fall in their money wealth as well as the steady erosion of the purchasing power of their interest receipts.

The opposite may well happen to holders of equity in companies; although a rise in nominal interest rates should have a depressing effect on share prices in the absence of inflation there are a number of offsetting factors in the situation postulated here. First is the reduced real burden of interest on old borrowings and rent on old leases, which would enable the firm to raise the real dividend paid out of given real profits. Second, the stock market, like the management, may be misled by the published accounts into thinking that real profits have risen. Finally, the share price should be equal to the present value of future real dividends discounted at the real interest rate and the latter, we have seen, has fallen. For these reasons a stock-market boom seems likely. However it cannot be sustained since all the factors referred to above are temporary, and the market will also have to cope, when it sees through the accounting conventions, with the problems for real profits of the increased real wage if that does indeed occur.

The upshot of all this is that in the transitional period there are likely to be substantial shifts in the distribution of income, and especially wealth. These shifts will generally be to the disadvantage of wealth owners especially if they do not have a well-diversified portfolio of fixed interest, equity, and real assets (such as houses). The change we are considering could be quite devastating to someone who holds nothing but long-term fixed-interest securities issued at the low interest rate appropriate to the era of stable prices: in the case of an undated 'consol' the ultimate interest-rate rise from 3 per cent to, say, 12 per cent involves the loss of three-quarters of the *money* value of his wealth. If this fall is spread over four years during which inflation takes place at 10 per cent p.a. his *real* wealth falls by seven-eighths and continues to fall at 10 per cent p.a. thereafter.

The situation is not significantly improved by the way the authorities often intervene to 'protect' people from the consequences of changes in the rate of interest. In the first place they tend to intervene on behalf of borrowers, even though real interest rates have fallen. The reason for this is no doubt that they are particularly concerned with the effects on mortgages, where there is a real problem for recent purchasers if interest rates rise sharply. However official restraint on mortgage-interest rates, if not effectively extended to other deposits, simply leads to a withdrawal of funds from the mortgage market, hence cutting house prices and building activity. This may be particularly disastrous for the very people the scheme was designed to help.

Suppose that in a stable economy the mortgage rate is 5 per cent. Suddenly everyone expects (correctly) inflation at 10 per cent so that the effective rate should rise to 15 per cent. But the authorities hold the rate to 10 per cent with the result that funds become scarce and house prices fall by, say, 20 per cent. Consider a young person who had just bought a £10,000 house on 90 per cent borrowed funds and whose repayments at 5 per cent were as much as he could afford. If the lending institution now raises his payments to those appropriate to a uniform money annuity at 10 per cent (as they are entitled to do under variable rate mortgages, as in Britain) his repayments would almost double, putting his budget under great strain. Selling the house for the £8,000 it will now fetch would not help very much since its price is now lower than the debt secured on it, and once the house is sold it may be difficult to borrow even one-tenth of its value as an unsecured loan. None of these inequities or hardships would arise if debt repayments were themselves escalated or indexed instead of being in fixed annual money terms.

Inflation and Price-Level Uncertainty

One effect of inflationary experience is to make people, whether as holders of long-term government debt or as recent house purchasers, acutely conscious of their vulnerability to the changes associated with changing price levels and interest rates. This consciousness itself almost certainly represents a significant loss of welfare, even if the redistribution of income and wealth away from property owners is not unwelcome. However the consequences of price-level uncertainty are more pervasive than this and, by inhibiting effective investment and therefore growth, also work to the disadvantage of the propertyless.

One might query whether inflation should really be blamed for the costs of price-level uncertainty. After all there is no immediate logical link between inflation, defined as a sustained change in the price level, and uncertainty about that change. Suppose the price index is 100 and everyone agrees that it is as likely to fall 5 per cent as to rise 5 per cent over the next year, then there is price-level uncertainty around a zero rate of expected inflation. If everyone thinks 110 the most likely level for next year but that it might be 105 or 115 with the same probability as previously attached to its being 95 or 105 we have expected inflation (of 10 per cent) but no increase in uncertainty. Why is it, then, that inflation does seem to reduce people's confidence in their ability to forecast prices?

A major reason is that even at high rates of inflation, the authorities nearly always announce high hopes for programmes whose intended affect is to bring the rate of inflation down rapidly. Thus with inflation at 20 per cent p.a. talk of bringing it down to 'below 10 per cent in two years' is quite common. On the other hand people are very sceptical of such claims; if they know that inflation tends to accelerate they may consider the possibility that it will rise to 30 per cent equally likely, especially if expectations are undergoing a 'change of gear' of the type described in Chapter VII.

These illustrative figures suggest that the rate of inflation might be considered equally likely to increase or decrease by one-half of its present amount, and that it is around this uncertain trend that a constant margin of error is allowed for. Such expectations would imply that price-level uncertainty, as measured by the variance of the expected rate of inflation, would increase almost proportionately with the square of the expected rate of inflation: at a 10-per-cent average expected rate of inflation it might be, perhaps, three times as great as at 5 per cent.

Effects of Price-Level Uncertainty

Whatever the precise mechanisms, there is very little room for doubt that some such process does take place, in which case we have to examine the consequence of increased uncertainty about future prices. The principal effect is to discourage people from entering into long-term monetary contracts, which both parties would now view as riskier, even if the money payments appropriate to a real rate of interest were specified to escalate additionally by the rate of inflation agreed to be the most likely. The lender would want more escalation and the borrower less to cover their respective risks; under this circumstance agreement will be difficult to reach. The contracts affected by these disincentives are all long-term contracts—and even a year becomes 'long' at a high and uncertain enough rate of inflation—relating to wages, loan agreements, and rental, hire, or leasing arrangements. In the case of wage agreements the employers can recover unexpected wage increases in higher prices; this asymmetry of risks may impart an upward bias to wage settlements.

The longest lending contracts most individuals make relate to their retirement; contributions to a pension fund are made up to forty years before retirement while the retirement annuity itself may, with luck, be drawn for twenty to thirty years. A life insurance policy may provide, directly or indirectly, for an annuity for as long as sixty years. Under stable prices long-term fixed-interest government securities offer an excellent way of making these provisions for the future. Inflation undermines this in two ways. First, it reduces real interest rates, at least transitionally, and thus reduces the pension or annuity that can be bought for a given contribution. Second, loss of confidence in future price levels mean that savers cannot calculate the provision they must make out of current income in order to provide any particular standard of living in their retirement, if the contributions are invested in fixed-interest stocks. The obvious solution would be to invest in long-dated indexed bonds, but these do not exist. Thus the arrangements for providing for one's retirement are substantially damaged by inflation as are the prospects of past savers whose pensions depend on institutional holdings of old fixed-interest securities.

There are several consequences of this deterioration of pension and annuity arrangements; one is that the inadequacy of private pensions resulting from the fall in the real value of old fixed interest securities, and the interest on them, may lead to pressure on the authorities to increase social-security pensions, especially for the higher-income groups who had previously made private arrangements. Since the indexed State pensions are typically financed out of current contributions, rather than out of past savings, the effect of substituting public for private pensions is to reduce the level of savings and capital formation, and thus the community's future productivity and real income. A second effect is that the absence of a market in annuities changes the behaviour of people with capital who in the past might have lived on an annuity and left virtually no estate. If annuities are unattractive, either on account of the low return they offer, or because they fail to offer real security, such people will tend to retain their capital in their own hands. If they are cautious about spending their capital, because of the risk of their living a long time, they may actually consume less, and leave more, thus raising the rate of savings, but also having an adverse effect on the distribution of wealth.

Businesses are also affected by the discouragement of long-term contracts resulting from price-level uncertainty. There are three possible responses to this uncertainty, and three types of cost. The first response is to make the same contracts you would under stable prices but to be miserable about it, to lose sleep, acquire ulcers, and so on. Much of this has been apparent in recent years but, as usual, the 'no change' response is not very likely to persist. If long contracts become less attractive people will make short ones; the standard period between rent reviews on commercial property in Britain has fallen from twenty-one, to seven, to five, and now to three years in the course of two decades of accelerating inflation. But this response too has its costs: as a shopkeeper I want to know what rent I shall have to pay for some time ahead if I am to try to build up a clientele in one location. The reason that there were long contracts in the absence of inflation was to provide this kind of assurance. Under inflation, with its attendant risks, one has either to write a long escalating contract and live with the fear that one has chosen the wrong escalation rate, or to enter into a short contract and run the risk that someone else will offer the landlord more (in real terms) when the time comes to renew. In the second case one would have to choose between paying the exorbitant rent or abandoning one's investment in building up the business.

The point of this little example is very general. Businesses have to commit themselves in their real activities to things that will pay off only after some time. The shopkeeper developing his trade is in the same situation as the industrialist laying down durable plant. Investment has to be financed, and if the risks of financial arrangements rise investment will be discouraged. However, in equilibrium, even an inflationary equilibrium, investment can fall only if savings are also deterred by price-level uncertainty. One way in which this might happen was mentioned when we discussed the effect of price-level uncertainty on pension arrangements. Even if saving, and hence the volume of investment, do not actually fall it is likely that the productivity of the investment would be reduced as a result of a reluctance to make long-term commitments. One could easily have a situation analogous to one in which instead of a long-term investment, like widening roads, so that buses can travel at 60 m.p.h. (in which case if each bus takes 50 people one bus provides 300 passenger miles per hour), all the investment goes into short-term investment, like buses which congest the narrow lane and travel at 10 m.p.h. so that five buses provide only 250 passenger miles per hour. The investment may be the same but the net output is still reduced. Thus even if consumption does not displace investment in the short run the concentration of investment in short-term projects will reduce its efficiency and ultimately output, savings, and investment.

Price-Level Uncertainty and the Cost of Finance

The following example shows that the risks of financing long-term investment rise with price-level uncertainty. Suppose that inflation is at 20 per cent p.a. while long and short interest rates are both at 15 per cent. What, one might think, could be more conducive to investment than a real-interest rate of *minus* 5 per cent? If the investment to be financed lasts twenty years one might expect to finance it with a twenty-year bond. This might present the cash-flow difficulties referred to in the previous chapter. However serious problems would remain even if there were *no* interim annual payments and the bond provided for the repayment twenty years hence of the principal compounded at 15 per cent p.a. £100 compounded (continuously) at 15 per cent for twenty years becomes £2,000, equivalent to merely £38 in terms of the initial purchasing power of money if there is inflation at 20 per cent p.a. for the twenty years. The reduction of £100 to £38 over twenty years represents a real rate of interest of *minus* 5 per cent p.a. But what would happen to our borrower if inflation which was 20 per cent last year did not continue but were to fall to 15 per cent this year, 10 per cent next year, and 5 per cent p.a. thereafter? The £2,000 would in that case be equivalent to an initial £600 which corresponds to a real rate of interest of (+)9 per cent p.a.

The central point about this example is that long-term real interest rates are not to be estimated by the long-term nominal rate, less the current rate of inflation. It is the course of inflation over the next twenty years that matters. And that is anybody's guess! Anyone who cannot guess is unlikely to be willing to invest if he has to finance his investment in this way. What are the alternatives?

One alternative is to borrow short: negative real short-term rates really are certainly negative. What can be questioned is the wisdom of borrowing short for a long-term investment. After all, if the initial loan is only for one year it will have to be renewed nineteen times or converted into a longer loan. Why should the real rate be −5 per cent next year? Even if it is, what guarantee is there that the bank will be willing to lend at the going rate? It might have been told to ration credit and that the industry in question does not have high priority.

Another alternative is not to get 'fixed interest finance' but to rely on equity capital. In that case there would still be two problems. First, the tax system in many countries favours debt interest over equity earnings so that equity capital is more expensive to firms. Price-level uncertainty then raises the cost of capital and thus deters investment. Secondly, even if there were no tax advantage, companies would choose to issue, and investors would choose to hold, a mixture of debt and equity on the general principle of portfolio balancing. People who believe they can assess the real risks of particular firms may even borrow at fixed interest in order to buy extra equity, while people who do not like such real risks would choose to hold bonds if they were confident about future prices. If that confidence declines then they must either put up with those risks or run down their investment.

Index-Linked Securities

Is there then no solution? In principle there is a solution, namely the *indexed bond*. An indexed bond is an ordinary bond except that each payment, whether of interest or principal, is adjusted in line with the change in some price index since the date of issue. It is often assumed that only the government could issue indexed bonds. But the preceding analysis suggests that private bodies have very real reasons for both issuing and holding such securities. They do in fact exist in a number of modest forms, particularly in rental contracts, but they are indeed rare. Why is this so?

The main problem lies in finding an acceptable index: in the old days such a contract would typically have been specified not in terms of a general index but in terms of one particular commodity, usually a staple commodity, like the corn in which Oxford colleges received rent for several centuries. Such indexation offers at best very partial protection of one's real income: it substitutes relative price uncertainty, the risk that corn will be cheap and the rent of low exchange value, for general price-level uncertainty. To overcome the inadequacy of a single-commodity index involves concocting a basket of goods. This raises a number of problems of definition and the treatment of quality change; is one 1970 bicycle equivalent to one 1870 penny-farthing, and are there not different models of both? Moreover baskets including foodstuffs will display seasonality which one would probably not want to reflect in the adjusted payments. It would be impossibly expensive to draw up detailed guidelines to cover all these points and to employ statisticians to compute the quarterly rental due on one property in this way. Even a major holder or issuer of contracts would find it difficult to justify such costs, though if the desire were strongly felt, a group of people could commission a body of independent statisticians.

More recently it has become possible to use officially published indices the compilers of which are experts in solving the definitional problems involved. Unfortunately, the authorities have been known, sometimes for quite good reasons, to allow the inevitable arbitrariness of the composition of such an index to reduce its representativeness. To rely on an official index in the face of inflation is to put one's faith in an authority which has in the past promised to prevent the inflation which creates the problem. This might even apply to a very broad index such as the Gross Domestic Product deflator; many people in the West are sceptical about the indices produced in Communist countries.

Another problem for a private indexed bond would be to meet the requirements of a bond for the purposes of the tax deduction usually extended to corporate 'interest' payments. If no restriction were imposed firms might be tempted to issue 'bonds' virtually identical to their equity, but qualifying for preferential tax treatment, by finding an index closely related to, if not defined in terms of, the companies' own profits. Thus the authorities would have to participate in any widespread indexation even if they did not initiate it or apply it to their own debt.

If one's own currency and government are not to be trusted one might try an index link to the currency of some foreign country whose authorities are more successful in maintaining price stability. Even here there are risks: exchange rates do not maintain purchasing-power parity and how would the contract be interpreted if trade controls and multiple exchange rates were introduced? Moreover who would willingly take on such liabilities? Only the producers of tradable goods have any reason to think in such terms and even for them the link could be broken by certain types of trade policy. Moreover the risks of such policies being adopted under the sorts of circumstances in which inflation threatens to get out of control are quite considerable.

A stable money is a very useful device and if confidence in it is destroyed it is not an easy task to concoct a substitute. Failing a substitute, the efficiency of the economy is likely to be reduced in two ways. First, as discussed in Chapter X, the efficiency of current transactions will be reduced as a result of people economizing in the means of exchange. This effect is likely to be relatively small before a flight from money sets in as it would under hyperinflation. Second, the absence of a convenient store of value in terms of which contracts can be made for future payment will, as argued above, inhibit long-term investment even at apparently low real rates of interest. These low real rates of return to savers penalize thrift and encourage consumption so that both the level and the productivity of investment are likely to fall.

Sources and Further Reading

GIERSCH, H., *et. al.*, *Essays on Inflation and Indexation*, Washington, D.C., 1974.
LIESNER and KING, op. cit.

XII INFLATION AND COUNTER-INFLATION: DIRECT CONTROLS

An Optimal Rate of Inflation

THE PRECEDING chapters emphasized the costs of inflation but also recognized some of its advantages—in particular the role of inflation as a tax on the services of money which might be an element in an optimal taxation structure. As such, it would almost certainly be a very slow inflation since inflation in excess of the real interest rate represents a tax of more than 100 per cent on the convenience yield of money and relatively few commodities should carry taxes at such a high rate. This suggests a rate of inflation of not more than 5 per cent p.a. Inflation at a lower rate than this might well also contribute to reducing the 'natural/normal' rate of unemployment, as was argued in Chapter VI, by reducing the effects of downward money-wage rigidity.

Friedman would not accept either of these arguments. He has argued that the optimal rate of inflation is actually negative,[1] with the problem of downward money-wage rigidity being partly offset by wage payments being linked to a price index.[2] His reason for preferring deflation is that it enables a positive real return to be earned on money holdings. This will encourage individuals to hold more cash balances and their increased liquidity will increase their satisfaction at no real cost since negligible real resources are involved in supplying them with paper tokens or mere book entries. Unless people's demand for liquidity can be satiated they will always prefer liquid money to illiquid real assets in the absence of an interest differential. Thus, if they are to hold both, as is surely desirable, the real return on money—the rate of deflation—must be less than the real return on physical assets. Indeed it must be less than the *net of tax* return on investment in physical assets. Arguments about the best rate of inflation thus all point to a range between *plus* and *minus* 5 per cent. In

[1] M. Friedman, *The Optimal Quantity of Money*, Chicago, Illinois, 1969.
[2] M. Friedman, *Monetary Correction*, London, 1974.

this chapter and the next we consider the problem of reducing inflation towards this target area.

Inflation and Direct Controls

Since the time of Diocletian (A.D. 245–313) authorities have tended to respond to rising prices by prohibiting them. Such a policy is suggested by cost-push theories of inflation, the elements of truth in which, it was argued above, are largely incidental to a more fundamental monetary process. It is possible that, taken out of this monetary context autonomous cost-push theories would suggest a policy of direct controls on prices and incomes to reduce inflation even if an inappropriate monetary policy were being pursued. Indeed, if controls on prices and wages are seen as an alternative to deflationary monetary policy, and especially if agreement to such an 'incomes' policy is conditional on an easing of monetary policy, it is quite possible that this approach to reducing inflation will in fact accelerate it. Because of this possible two-way relationship between inflation and attempts at direct controls of it, we discuss this policy before discussing alternative approaches in the next chapter.

The possibility of controls being ineffective, or worse, depends on three considerations: first, that they may constitute a 'cover' behind which an irresponsible monetary policy is pursued; second, they may temporarily raise the natural rate of unemployment and thus render inflationary an otherwise neutral or deflationary monetary policy; finally, even if a neutral monetary policy is pursued, they might bring about only a temporary fall in inflation. The relevance of the first consideration is obvious if one accepts the third. The second proposition is also straightforward.

For reasons which will become apparent when the third proposition is discussed, 'incomes policies' may nowadays, unlike Diocletian's, be the outcome of a 'bargain' between the authorities imposing the controls and the bodies, especially trade unions, whose behaviour is to be controlled. We have already noted that this bargain may involve an expansionary monetary policy designed to maintain employment. Another element in the bargain with the unions may be a redistribution of income. If such redistribution took the form of an increase in the progressivity of the personal tax structure it would probably do little harm. It might have disincentive effects on the labour supply, either of those who find that their standard of living can rise even if they work less, or of those who see no point in working so hard if they can keep less of what they earn. This would have the effect of reducing equilibrium output, and thus raising prices. However, negotiating in the context of a 'pay policy' the parties are liable to settle on a formula which provides for larger increases in the pre-tax money wages of lower-paid employees than for tax changes.

Such a policy involves a change in relative real wages, employers' wage costs, and probably an increase in the *real* wages of the lowest paid. These in turn will imply changes in the equilibrium distribution of employment. In this respect an incomes policy becomes comparable with a technological change, or a change in the terms of trade, and is equally likely to generate unemployment especially among the low paid. Recent British measures such as £1+4 per cent (1973) flat-rate increases related to the cost of living (1974's threshold payments), and a uniform £6 a week (1975–6) have all had this feature. Following one another in quick succession they may have had a major cumulative effect in the substitution of relatively highly paid men servicing tea-vending machines for the low-paid women who used to serve tea. The scope for such substitution is very considerable in all but the very short run. Moreover, the redistribution of income will also change demand patterns as the poor, whose incomes rise, will not buy the same goods as the rich stop buying. Unskilled suppliers of labour-intensive services to the rich thus find the demand for their services reduced as a result of both income and substitution effects on the part of their customers, to whom their higher wages appear as high prices, as well as substitution of capital or skilled labour for their own by their employers. These effects could be quite important if one starts from a high rate of inflation. Consider, for example, an incomes policy of a uniform increment equal to 10 per cent of the average wage and suppose that prices are expected to rise by 10 per cent so that average real income will be unchanged. Then the wage of someone initially earning half the average will be raised by 20 per cent in money terms and 10 per cent in real terms while someone earning twice the average has a 5-per-cent money increase and a 5-per-cent real fall.

Even if we ignore any effects on the pattern of demand for products, a unit elasticity of demand for low-paid labour, with respect to its real wage, would imply a 10-per-cent fall in demand for the services of those initially paid half the average, and about 3 per cent for those paid three-quarters of the average. If there are twice as many people with wages between the average and three-quarters of it (of whom $1\frac{1}{2}$ per cent become unemployed) as between three-quarters and one-half of the average wage (of whom 7 per cent might lose their jobs) about $1\frac{1}{2}$ per cent of the working population is liable to join the unemployed. Against this must be set the increase in the demand for the services of the relatively highly paid. If the distribution of skills of the initially unemployed had the normal heavy weighting of low-skill/low-pay people the chances of meeting this increased demand from that source would be slight.

It may, of course, be argued that few anti-inflationary pay policies prescribe minimum-pay rates (although many countries do have minimum wage laws) and that the preceding mechanistic analysis of a policy of flat-rate increases therefore exaggerates its effect. While this is true, those who insist on such redistributive clauses in the policies presumably believe that they have some effect on relative wages. To the extent that their beliefs are correct the policy will generate additional unemployment. It is important to stress that this argument does not depend on the belief that either the initial wage structure or the initial income distribution was itself either in full equilibrium or 'right'. It depends only on the assumption that an arbitrary disturbance to the system is more likely to move it further away from equilibrium and thus generate unemployment, than to do the opposite. One could therefore reject the argument if one had reason to believe that a general reduction of wage differentials was a movement towards equilibrium. This is a possibility but it has not been argued by the advocates of such policies. They place more emphasis on 'justice' than on equilibrium, and in this context seem to prefer controls to taxes as a means of enforcing it.

The third proposition put forward above was that prices and incomes policies would bring about only a temporary fall in inflation. Their capacity to do even that is important and would imply that they might have a part to play in reducing the cost of other methods of lowering the rate of inflation by facilitating a rapid reduction of inflation expectations. This possibility is pursued further in the next chapter. Here we consider the effects of such a policy in isolation from other measures.

'Prices and incomes' policies consist of packages whose structure reflects the current emphasis of political and economic analysis. They rarely consist exclusively of price *or* wage controls but, frequently, one set of controls is designed to be effective while the other is largely a monitoring, or even a 'cosmetic', device. One can therefore analyse the two components separately. We start, as Diocletian did, with price controls.

Price Controls

If the price control takes the form of a 'freeze', without reference to costs, any increase in money wages becomes an increase in real wages. This tends to result in rising unemployment, falling output, and growing shortages since demand is unlikely to fall as rapidly as does output. If there was no initial excess demand, shortages would not emerge until the squeeze on profitability from rising real wages reduced demand for labour. The consequent fall in output would exceed the reduction in demand for goods and services.

Sooner or later excess demand will occur despite the falling employment. Domestic shortages may be met by imports, if they are not subject to controls, in which case exchange depreciation may make uncontrolled exports more profitable than controlled domestic sales. The net effect does not only lead to inefficiency as trade flows are distorted between countries but also to an increase in both unemployment and the price of imported goods. Moreover, the reduction in profits and profitability of production for the home market is likely to reduce investment, jeopardizing future growth and productivity.

Thus, even if the policy is successful in restraining the rise in the domestic selling prices of domestic products, and is not nullified by black markets, which might develop in response to the shortages, it has damaging side effects which render it unsustainable unless aggregate demand is being cut simultaneously. Otherwise the economy's real position will detriorate even if the rate of growth of money wages abates. A redistribution of income from profits to wages will have taken place which will have to be reversed either directly or by fiscal measures, if investment is to be resumed. One possibility would be to increase pay-roll taxes on employees and reduce them on employers. This would tend to restore both employment and investment, but if this tax change is an integral part of the scheme the policy cannot be described simply as a price policy since an indirect wage control has become central to it.

A prices policy which aims to 'freeze' not prices but the margins by which producers' selling prices exceed the cost of their direct inputs would have no effect if the inflation was already in equilibrium and margins were frozen, in proportion, at their equilibrium level. If, however, the inflation was tending to accelerate much would depend on the type of margins controlled. Fixed historic cost margins imply lower real margins at higher rates of inflation.

Thus, the fixed historic cost margin case is similar, if inflation is accelerating, to an attempt to reduce real margins and would have effects similar to those of price level control. Even if inflation were not accelerating, real margins might be frozen at an unsustainable level to which they had been reduced as a result of producers' slowness to abandon historic margins. They would slow down inflation only by distorting the economy and getting it into an unsustainable situation as far as the balance of real wages, consumption and investment were concerned, at the same time as raising unemployment. It is possible that the unemployment generated in this way would tend to reduce the rate of increase of money wages and prices, as also would any effect of the measures on inflation expectations—effects which might arise either directly from the implementation of the policy or from its effects on recorded prices. If, however, the rising unemployment led the authorities to abandon or relax the controls, inflation would pick up again unless the balance of monetary aggregate demand and supply had shifted towards excess supply during the period of controls.

Wage Controls

Direct controls on wages do not suffer from these disadvantages because, although a redistribution of income *towards* profits may be objectionable, being more easily reversible it is less likely to have very damaging economic effects. It may worsen labour relations but these are as likely to deteriorate as a result of direct resentment against the wage controls in the public sector as from resentment at any increase in profits in the private sector. Moreover, if the main burden of control falls on wages, back-up controls on real profit margins would be harmless. As long as wage controls did not disturb *relative* wages, one would not expect wage restriction, which would tend to reduce real wages, to generate unemployment, although it is possible that labour supply, and hence output and the domestic demand for it, would fall.

There is, however, another difference between price and wage controls which works to the disadvantage of the latter. Both controls attempt to impose on voluntary transactions terms other than those the parties would have agreed if left to themselves. If a transaction would be mutually advantageous at the uncontrolled price (and if it were not it would not take place) why should it not remain so? How does the policy affect agreed prices?

The simple answer is that one party or the other is subject to legal sanctions. The effectiveness of such sanctions depends on legal or institutional obstacles to a black market when shortages become apparent. A black market, as a separate market, is rather difficult to imagine in the case of labour. However the argument about controls being an attempt to impose a solution other than that which would emerge naturally is more directly applicable in a situation of face-to-face bargaining.

The natural response to wage controls is for the parties to negotiate first on the basis that the controls do not exist and, subsequently, having agreed terms (on which their interests *do* conflict) to turn their minds *jointly* to reconciling their agreement with the terms of the controls. The controls will almost certainly have loop-holes for promotion, upgrading, restructuring, etc., which will not present great difficulties if the parties co-operate.

Although in this sense wage controls are unlikely to be very effective, it is possible that their announcement will, as a result of the effect of the policy on inflation expectations, affect the terms of the bargains, at the first stage of the procedure described above. This is most likely to occur if people do not recognize the scope for circumventing the policy. This in turn is most likely to be the case if such policies have not been discredited in the recent past, which in its turn probably requires that they should not have been much resorted to by governments.

Although we have argued that, legal liability notwithstanding, wage controls are unlikely to be very effective in the private sector, the situation is rather different in the public sector where a general conspiracy to defeat the objectives of policy is more difficult to organize. Regrading and other devices would rapidly become notorious if built into the much publicized agreements in the public sector; in any case the government will probably bring direct pressure to bear on public-sector negotiators not to cheat in this way. Thus, the effectiveness of the controls in the public sector is likely to be tested by direct confrontation on the issue of the legal sanctions (if any) underlying the policy. If the policy is ineffective in the private sector, the government is liable to be seen to be using legal sanctions against public-sector employees in order to enforce 'unfair' settlements—an argument used with varying success by postal workers and miners in recent years.

As the enforcement of legal sanctions on trade unions (either directly on their members or their leaders) is difficult, unpopular, and ineffective (even in the United States where it does occasionally occur), we may be left with only two options. First, a short sharp freeze has usually been effective; the rot sets in with the attempt to organize an orderly 'thaw', or 're-entry'. Such a stage is called for at the end of the freeze, if either excess demand or inflationary expectations makes a resurgence of inflation probable. The second remaining possibility is 'voluntary restraint.'

There are two arguments underlying attempts to control inflation through voluntary restraint: (i) that complusion would probably not work for the reasons sketched above; and (ii) that rational men will agree to restrain their demands if they can be made to recognize that these demands are sustaining an inflationary process which they all dislike. The weaknesses of this argument are apparent. First, as argued in Chapter X, there are fewer reasons for men on the shop floor to deplore the effects of inflation than there are for either politicians or the media whose apparent unanimity may be deceptive. Second, the argument that, if only decent people see what is in their collective interest, they can be expected to agree to do it, and to abide by that agreement, regardless of incentives for individuals, is seductive but unconvincing.

If this argument, which elevates Kant's categorical imperative from an appealing *moral principle* to an implausible *description* of economic agents, were true, the world would be a much better place. Everybody would recognize that buses can only run if people pay fares; therefore, they could be relied upon to pay without incurring the costs of employing a conductor (or requiring the driver to do the conductor's job). Unfortunately, people also know that as long as the buses are running one can consume more of other things if one does *not* pay the fare, and one's own failure to do so will not significantly affect the viability, and hence the availability, of the service.

Uncongested buses and price stability are both examples of 'public goods'. These are goods and services which everyone can enjoy equally if they are provided, and which therefore each person has an interest (perhaps a immoral interest) in trying to persuade others to provide but no interest in paying for himself. The problem is well known as that of the 'free rider', an apt enough description in the case of the buses. It is one familiar to trade unionists in their arguments against non-members who enjoy the benefits of union-negotiated rates without contributing to the strike fund which strengthened the union's bargaining position when negotiating those rates.

The argument about the general good would not involve this problem if there were central negotiations by monolithic organizations. However, this does not really provide a solution, although it seems to work in Sweden and Austria, because, even if central negotiations take place, the labour representatives have to enforce their side of the bargain on individual groups who could get a better deal on their own. The centrally negotiated wages may not be any easier to enforce than a statutory policy, and the central labour organization is unlikely to have as many powers as the government which, as we have seen, would probably find its own inadequate.

Sources and Further Reading

BARRO, R. J., and GROSSMAN, H. I., 'Suppressed Inflation and the Supply Multiplier', *Review of Economic Studies*, January 1974.

CLEGG, H. A., *How to Run an Incomes Policy and Why We Made Such a Mess of the Last One*, London, 1971.

MEADE, J. E., *An Intelligent Radical's Guide to Economic Policy*, London, 1975.

PARKIN, J. M., and SUMNER, M., (eds.), *Incomes Policy and Inflation*, Manchester, 1972.

ULMAN, L., and FLANAGAN, R. J., *Wage Restraint: Incomes Policies in W. Europe*, London, 1971.

XIII DEFLATION, WAGE INDEXATION, AND CRISIS MEASURES

The Monetarist Package

IF INCOMES policies inspired by theories of autonomous cost push are unlikely to achieve voluntary acceptance, are unlikely to be legally enforceable, and are liable to cause serious distortions which render them unsustainable in the long run, what are the prospects for the policies inspired by more monetary theories? Most monetarists have emphasized that had their prescriptions been followed, inflation would never have become the serious problem it now is. This claim may be plausible but is inevitably both untestable and unhelpful in the context of any particular inflationary situation.

The central tenet of the monetarist faith is that the real economy is inherently stable—with a tendency to full employment—but that this equilibrium is liable to be dislocated by monetary disturbances. This explains the monetarists' fear of rapid changes in monetary conditions in either direction—monetarists tend to be gradualists—and this in turn explains their reluctance to prescribe crisis measures even for inflation others regard as being of crisis proportions. Thus we consider below the possibility of complementing the basic monetarist strategy with more drastic temporary measures.

What would be the consequences of adopting gradual monetary contraction at a time when the rate of inflation was high (over 10 per cent p.a.) and when many people expected it to rise?

Reduction in the Growth of the Money Supply

The first item of the monetarist package would be the reduction of the growth rate of some monetary aggregate over a number of years starting from a figure lower than the current rate of inflation. Money-supply growth at the previous rate of inflation would tend to sustain it, or to slow it only by the two or three percentage points a year of real-output growth. If the previous inflation rate was rising it is likely that expectations had not adjusted fully. Then the fall in desired real balances, as expectations adapted, might well more than offset the effects of real income growth, so that inflation might actually accelerate temporarily if the money supply continued to rise at the rate of the previous inflation.

If monetary growth were to be cut in this way, without any complementary fiscal policy, the authorities would have to make larger sales of interest-bearing debt than they would otherwise have done and this would tend to raise nominal interest rates. It is, however, possible that the monetary restriction would cause people to revise downwards their expectations of inflation, and, thus, make them more willing to hold long-term fixed-interest debt. Even if this last factor prevented nominal rates rising much—if at all—the evidence suggests that such a policy would raise real interest rates quite sharply. The point can be illustrated by reference to the argument of Chapter XI. Suppose that the interest rate on twenty-year bonds is 15 per cent p.a. with inflation at 25 per cent p.a.; monetary restrictions are introduced and inflation is expected to fall to zero in five years. If the nominal rate is unchanged, the real cost of capital rises, initially, to over $(+)10$ per cent p.a., and even if the adjustment took ten years, it would rise to 7 per cent.

The effect of such increases in real interest rates would almost certainly be to reduce investment substantially—and hence both income and employment. It was suggested in Chapter XI that an indexed bond might ease a company's problems of uncertainty in such a situation but it would not necessarily reduce the expected real rate of interest. If the authorities wanted to prevent the concentration of the effects of deflation on investment activity they would have also to vary some other item in their over-all budget and financing arrangements—not merely the balance of interest- and non-interest-bearing debt—they must reduce the budget deficit (or raise the surplus). The purpose of this is not to prevent the initial fall in income and employment associated with the purely monetary deflationary policy but to spread the effects over industries other than capital-goods industries and to reduce the long-term damage to the economy's productive capacity.

A deficit can be reduced either by expenditure cuts or by increased tax revenue. If revenue is to be raised, it can be raised either by raising direct taxes on incomes, or by raising indirect taxes (including the prices of products supplied by the public sector and public enterprise). The fact that indirect taxes raise the prices paid by consumers and are in that sense inflationary (even though aggregate demand is reduced) is well known. It is also possible that they thereby have a damaging effect on expectations and, for both reasons, on wages. We have already seen in Chapter IX that raising direct taxes is also liable to increase wage demands and thus to contribute to cost inflationary pressures. What, then, about cutting public expenditure?

Reductions in Government Expenditure

That many 'monetarists' have an ideological predilection for this remedy is unquestionable; however, they also have reasons which deserve to be taken seriously. First, they point to the weaknesses of the alternatives we have just considered. Second, if one has started from an optimal level of public expenditure, one should be indifferent at the margin between public expenditure and the alternative private uses to which the resources could be put. The welfare cost of cutting public expenditure is not the value of the output but the *difference* between the value of the results of public and private use of the resources. At the margin there should be no such difference. Moreover, if public expenditure has been financed by the creation of money, the authorities may have believed that the economy required reflating. In which case they may have indulged in 'make work' public projects such as the construction of Lansbury's Lido in Hyde Park in 1930. Such projects are often justified by the argument that the opportunity cost of unemployed labour is less than the wage that it is paid. However, if inflation follows such a programme the level of of full employment has been misjudged and the programme should be cut. Alternatively, the authorities may have been determined to undertake certain expenditures although they did not believe that they had adequate public support for non-inflationary tax finance. If they were right that the electorate would not choose to support the expenditure with tax money, then it seems appropriate that the inflation following the monetary expansion should be curbed by cutting the expenditure whose constitutional propriety is in doubt.

For these reasons a monetarist would urge monetary restraint combined with reduced public expenditure—both to be gradual. What would be the consequences of such a policy? In part its consequences will depend on the way the policy is presented, and the credibility of this presentation. In particular the amount of unemployment associated with a given rate of deceleration of monetary growth will depend on whether the announcement of the strategy has any direct effect on inflation expectations. If it does, then wage settlements, and therefore price increases, might abate independently of any increase in unemployment which may also be expected. In general, however, such expectations can only be justified if there is some other 'harder' mechanism operating in the same direction and, in the monetarist framework, this can only be unemployment. We have already seen that monetary restriction would tend to raise unemployment, whether through its effects on investment, unless the policy generated a great increase in confidence, or as a result of public expenditure cuts.

Wage Indexation

Provided that money-wage increases do respond to unemployment this strategy will work in the end, but several questions are raised by this gradualist approach; questions related to the probable cost of the stabilization programme. The first question is how long it will take. If real interest rates are raised by fairly rapid deflation there may be a virtual cessation of investment during the adjustment process: this suggests that the cost of gradualism may be high. Indexation of wages might also play a part in reducing the cost of the unemployment along such a path of gradual adjustment. If no attempt is made to present the policy in such a way as to operate directly on expectations a determined deflationary policy is almost bound to be more successful than expected in the sense that prices will rise less than people expected when making wage bargains. This means that *ex-post* real wages exceed planned real wages and employers will react by reducing employment. If the authorities knew that their policy would reduce inflation at a certain rate they could announce the path of prices, and, if they were believed, the amount of unemployment along the path would be substantially reduced. However, neither of these conditions is likely to be met. Thus, wage indexation is the only way to reduce the unemployment cost of unexpectedly successful deflation.

To argue in this way, as Friedman does,[1] for the inclusion of wage indexation in a deflationary package is not to argue that indexation

[1] See, e.g., *Monetary Correction*, London, 1974. Also R. Jackman, and K. Klappholz, *Taming the Tiger*, London, 1975.

on its own would do anything to slow inflation. Indeed it is easy to see that the effect of indexation is to eliminate the role of price expectations. Since there are times when the stickiness of price expectations reduces the inflationary response to excess demand, it is clear that where there is excess demand indexation may well accelerate inflation. Not only do the effects of wage indexation depend crucially on whether there is excess demand or supply; they also depend on whether the indexation is introduced at a time when real wages are above their equilibrium level (as might be the case after a deterioration in the terms of trade), or when a balanced inflation is being sustained by the momentum of expectations. In the latter case indexation would undoubtedly reduce the unemployment cost of 'purging' the system of its inflationary expectations. In the former case, however, while indexation overcomes the expectations problem, it may make the fundamental adjustment more difficult. This is especially true if the indexation is not in voluntary, renegotiable contracts but becomes, effectively, a government commitment to maintain an unsustainable real-income level. If the government is to be a party to indexation it is important that the index chosen is such that the possibility of reducing real disposable incomes is retained. This can be done by building into the index adjustments for indirect taxes and subsidies and changes in the terms of trade. For this purpose an index of output prices at the wholesale stage has obvious advantages over an index of consumer prices at the retail stage.

Minimizing the Unemployment Cost of Deflation

These problems of the transition are of some interest but are almost trivial compared to the major objection to the gradualist approach. We have seen that the costs of inflation can be exaggerated. The major costs arise from the fear that the system is liable to get out of control. Once this fear is allayed by the authorities making clear their determination, and willingness, to exert control, the relative benefits of reducing inflation over three years rather than five, or even ten, are probably slight. The economic variable whose course contributes most to the cost of stabilization is unemployment, yet the monetarist gradualists are, quite properly, very reluctant to predict the path of unemployment associated with their policies. The monetarist proposition that the lags in the system are long and variable which, as we saw in Chapter III, can be explained in terms of the role of expectations and speculation, implies that precision in this forecast is impossible.

This suggests that the authorities should attempt to ascertain the likely course of inflation in response to alternative paths of unemployment. Then, having chosen a path along which expected costs for the two together are minimized, they should try to adhere to an unemployment plan rather than a monetary plan—fiscal as well as monetary instruments being used to influence aggregate demand with a view to keeping the economy on the planned unemployment course. The advantage of this approach is not that unemployment is easier to control than the money supply (which is untrue) nor that the unemployment strategy provides a more reliable control over inflation (as we saw at the end of Chapter IX the natural rate may be liable to shift). The advantage lies in this being a feasible gradualist deflationary strategy immune from one serious weakness of the conventional monetarist strategy of choosing a path for the money supply and hoping for the best. The danger of this narrowly monetary approach is that, if unemployment rises more than expected, which may well happen, political pressures are likely to be generated leading to the abandonment of the experiment. Any such abandonment would be very costly in that, by undermining confidence in the authorities' capability and determination, it would make it almost impossible for their future policies to have beneficial direct effects on expectations. The alternative strategy of defining a target path for unemployment, though liable to be condemned as 'cold-blooded', minimizes this risk and thus lowers the expected unemployment cost of the ultimate reduction of inflation.

What would the least (unemployment) cost-path for stabilizing prices look like? Unfortunately we do not know; but there are some relevant considerations to bear in mind. If every man-month of unemployment made the same contribution to stabilization, then, given the initial level of inflation, one could compute the total number of man-months of unemployment (N) necessary to stop inflation. The question would then be whether one preferred to have N men unemployed for one month, or one man (not, of course, necessarily the same one) unemployed for N months. Assuming that it would not be the same man (or men), people who are not very impatient for stabilization might well opt for relatively little unemployment for quite a long time. This obviously accords with any general preference for gradualism. It has also been argued that the marginal employee (assuming the right one gets laid off) either values his employment relatively little or contributes relatively little to output. Thus the social cost of having two men unemployed is (slightly) higher than twice the cost of the first. Since, *ex hypothesi*, their unemployment contributes equally to price stabilization, the first man's unemployment is more 'cost-effective' than the second.

Sharp Deflation versus Gradualism

We have already argued that through its effects on real interest rates, investment, and so on, a long-drawn-out deflation may be more costly, in the long run, than a sharp one, although these costs could be reduced by indexation. The cost of indexation, and the impatience of politicians, both point to a short sharp crunch. Indeed, it may not be only the politicians who are impatient. If the electors believe the situation is critical they are liable to call for crisis measures. This is a demand which does not accord well with a gradualist plan to raise unemployment slightly and wait for a generation. It is also an open question whether each man-month of unemployment *does* make the same contribution to reducing inflation. It may be that the benefit is proportional to the cost; if only the least productive and least enthusiastic workers are unemployed, will the downward pressure on wage increases be very great? If the stabilizing benefit of unemployment is proportional to its social cost then the previous argument fails. Stabilization from a given level of inflation by this method has a fixed cost regardless of the time taken. In this case any impatience, or desire for crisis measures, would again point to a rather sharp deflation.

Indeed it is arguable that the idea of a 'salutary shock' is not entirely out of place here, especially as far as expectations are concerned. Keynes himself, discussing advice he had given along these lines at the time of the post-World War I inflation, wrote in 1942 that he stood by that advice—at least if direct controls were ruled out. He recommended 'a swift and severe dose of dear money, sufficient to break the market [expectations? JSF], and quick enough to prevent at least some of the disastrous consequences which would otherwise ensue'.[2] These 'disastrous consequences' include the possibility that

[2] See S. Howson, ' "A Dear Money Man?" Keynes on Monetary Policy 1920', *Economic Journal*, June 1973.

with a very gradualist policy people might become used to the higher levels of unemployment, which would ceased to dampen the rate of wage increase. It is quite possible that what determines wage increases is in part the level of unemployment relative to an experience-related 'norm'. In such a case the gradualist strategy would be both ineffective and very damaging to the country's long-term growth prospects as it would have an adverse effect, persisting for a generation, on future employment, as well as on investment, and thus on both output and living standards.

While these arguments point to a short sharp deflation it could hardly be of N men for one month. Two factors limit the feasibility of a crisis strategy. First, even if we know N we do not know what policies will induce the unemployment of N men for one month. Thus, some groping by the authorities is inevitable with respect both to the effect of policy on unemployment, and with respect to the effect of unemployment on inflation. The ignorant have no alternative to groping in the dark: can anything be said about optimal groping?

One result to which we referred when discussing union strategies in Chapter XI suggests that ignorance about the effects of policies is a reason not for caution but rather for making radical changes because they provide the most information. Suppose you are flying a helicopter from east to west (in uncharted country) at night searching for a man who has had an accident on the top of a ridge running north–south. You know that he is on your latitude and believe, but are not at all sure, that the ridge is about 20 miles ahead. What is the best search strategy? A cautious strategy might be to move 5 miles ahead. If the ground is still sloping upwards go another 5 miles, until the ground is found to slope downwards, then work backwards 1 mile at a time, and so on. An alternative, and more efficient, strategy is to fly 25 miles on the first trip. If the ground is still sloping upwards you have saved five steps. If it is sloping downwards, as it will be if the ridge is in fact 20 miles ahead, you can come back 6 and in two steps have restricted the search to a 6-mile range whereas the 'cautious' strategy took five steps to restrict it to a 5-mile range.

Along these lines it can be argued that under ignorance gradualism is inefficient. The authorities should err on the side of excess deflation. If they overshoot they can always come back and will have acquired valuable information about the behaviour of the economy in regions not explored in living memory.

However, there are two serious flaws in this argument. First, it ignores the delays before the consequences of policies reveal themselves. Our helicopter pilot had only to hop out at each landing-place and observe the direction in which the ground sloped in order to discover whether he had gone too far—no such simple test is available to the Chancellor of the Exchequer. Second, it ignores the problems involved in trying to exploit the possibility of influencing expectations more cheaply than by throwing men out of work. A relatively gradual policy may meet both these objections. If one starts with small doses of a medicine which is known to have a delayed effect, information on the patient's tolerance may become available before the dosage is raised too far. In addition, assuming that the early stages of the strategy have some success in curbing inflation, albeit at the cost of some unemployment, the cost-effectiveness of the subsequent stages will be increased by the policy's rising credibility.

Thus, having argued earlier that a pure gradualist strategy is too slow, we have shown that there are severe limitations on the speed with which a deflationary (or disinflationary) policy can be pursued, at least in the absence of wage indexation (which might be a mixed blessing), unless some other measure can be introduced to operate directly on expectations. Attempts to 'talk down' the rate of inflation are almost bound to be counter-productive in that their main effect is to discredit the speakers.

A Role for Wage/Price Controls

Could a temporary wage or price 'freeze', of the kind that history suggests is feasible, make a contribution in this context? The answer is almost certainly yes, in the circumstances in which indexation would also work. Namely when the real wage is not excessive and the inflation is being maintained by its own expectational momentum. Under these conditions a mandatory uniform ceiling on proportionate pay increases, not necessarily at a zero rate, as with a strict 'freeze', but obviously at less than the going rate of inflation, and probably backed up with a monitoring of profit margins, would reduce inflation almost at once. If it were also accompanied by deflationary measures, so that there was higher unemployment at the end of the 'partial freeze' than at the beginning and the government made it clear that unemployment would probably be allowed to rise further (and would certainly have to if inflation were to pick up again), then there is a real possibility that a discrete reduction in the rate of inflation, say by a third of its initial level (from 30 to 20 per cent or from 20 to 13 or from 12 to 8 per cent), could be achieved within a year at relatively low cost.

It is, however, absolutely vital that the two elements of direct control and deflation be recognized as complementary. If the *quid pro quo* for the unions' acquiescence in the 'freeze' were *no* increase in unemployment, then the programme would again serve to discredit a potentially useful device unless the initial level of unemployment were high. On the other hand the authorities could negotiate on the basis that with the 'freeze' a very much smaller increase in unemployment would be necessary than in its absence. Any such negotiations would be unlikely to be fruitful unless the authorities had already established as credible their determination to reduce the rate of inflation by unaided deflation—and unemployment—if necessary.

This solution may not be available to a country (such as Britain in 1974) which has recently suffered a deterioration in its terms of trade, so that its real wage is too high. In addition, monetary and exchange rate policies converted Britain's terms of trade deterioration into rapid inflation. What should such a country do? If no reduction of the real wage is feasible—or is only feasible at a social cost deemed to be excessive—the authorities can maintain the real *absorption* associated with full employment at the given real wage by running a trade deficit. However to maintain full employment at the given real wage will require assistance to employers which, we suggested above, could best be done by cutting their pay-roll taxes such as National Insurance contributions. If the authorities choose this second option, their only remaining problem is the inherited inflation sustained by the momentum of expectations and past mistakes in monetary and exchange-rate policy. To the extent that this 'hangover' inflation exceeds the amount which may be desirable (on the argument of Chapter VIII) to facilitate the reallocation of labour in response to the change in relative prices, it could then be tackled by the combination of a partial wage 'freeze' and appropriately deflationary monetary policy.

However the decision not to cut real absorption should not be lightly made. In particular, no government can pretend that a permanent deterioration in the terms of trade can leave both the current level and the prospective growth of real absorption unaffected. The choice is whether to forego a little now or, if international borrowing is at a positive real interest rate, more later.

Epilogue

Most countries have experienced rapid inflation from time to time. This book provides the economic half of a possible explanation. The notion, introduced in Chapter VII, that people use simple rules of thumb that have not recently been misleading is not restricted to consumers: it applies also to both economists and politicians. In a time of price stability workers' and consumers' price expectations become sluggish; politicians learn that expansionary policies reduce unemployment and raise output. Even if they know that they are storing up trouble for later this option is attractive to a politician nearing an honourable retirement whose interests do not extend beyond the next election.[3] The process of inflating before elections can be repeated several times if expectations are sluggish enough; but there are reasons for doubting whether it can be repeated indefinitely.

On the assumption that voters' expectations are also rational, in the weak sense, they will eventually learn that inflation follows the pre-election boom. When this lesson is learnt they are in a position to impose their time preference on politicians whose rational self-interest may make them short-sighted. Moreover, the electorate's learning about the relationship between boom and inflation is facilitated by the fact that the sensitization of their price expectations reduces the lags between causes and effects.

By the time it ceases to be easy to fool the electorate inflation will be endemic. The politicians may also learn only from experience that their old tricks no longer work. If they thus try two or three electoral booms after the public wakes up both rapid inflation and political disenchantment set in.

Popular demand for the reduction of the established rate of inflation leads to a political contest as to who can best slow it down. The difficulty of fulfilling the commitments politicians make in this process is liable to lead to further disenchantment, which may make some approaches to the task harder. However, despite these problems the existence of a fairly reliable, if unpleasant, method means that

[3] See W. Nordhaus, 'A Political Business Cycle', *Review of Economic Studies*, April 1975.

relative stability will probably be re-established in the end. In this case expectations will eventually become sufficiently sluggish for it to be politically attractive to start the whole process all over again—assuming that democracy survives the disenchantments.

INDEX